Haunted
Vermont

Haunted Vermont

Ghosts and Strange Phenomena
of the Green Mountain State

Charles A. Stansfield Jr.

Illustrations by Heather Adel Wiggins

STACKPOLE
BOOKS

Published by
STACKPOLE BOOKS
5067 Ritter Road
Mechanicsburg, PA 17055
www.stackpolebooks.com

Printed in the United States of America

10 9 8 7 6 5 4 3

FIRST EDITION

Design by Beth Oberholtzer
Cover design by Caroline Stover

Library of Congress Cataloging-in-Publication Data

Stansfield, Charles A.
    Haunted Vermont: ghosts and strange phenomena of the Green Mountain State / Charles A. Stansfield Jr.
       p.   cm.
    Includes bibliographical references.
    ISBN-13: 978-0-8117-3399-1 (pbk.)
    ISBN-10: 0-8117-3399-8 (pbk.)
    1. Ghosts–Vermont. 2. Haunted place–Vermont. 3. Parapsychology–Vermont. I. Title.
BF1472.U6S728   2007
133.109743—dc22   2006034011

To my nearest and dearest—
Diane, Wayne, Paul,
Beth, Jordan, Aidan, and Bryce
and
To all those fortunate enough
to call Vermont their home

Contents

Contents

Introduction

THE GREEN MOUNTAIN STATE CAN BE DIVIDED INTO FIVE REGIONS IN order to organize stories, its ghosts, and strange happenings on a geographic basis. The Green Mountains form a ruggedly beautiful spine running north and south. These mountains are flanked by lower elevations to both east and west. To the east is the valley of the Connecticut River, which forms the boundary with New Hampshire. On the western flanks of the Green Mountains, Lake Champlain forms more than half of Vermont's boundary with New York State.

The Green Mountains have been divided into two large regions, north and south. The northern Green Mountains region runs from the Canadian border to Roxbury and includes Montpelier, the state capital, and Barre, the famous granite quarrying center.

The southern Green Mountains encompass the scenic backbone south of Roxbury to the Massachusetts line and includes such famous Vermont locales as Rutland, Killington, Bennington, and Plymouth.

The Connecticut Valley region runs north from the Massachusetts border past Brattleboro, Windsor, and White River Junction to McIndoe Falls on the Connecticut River.

The Lake Champlain region runs from U.S. Highway 4 near Castleton northward to the Canadian border and includes Vergennes; Vermont's largest city, Burlington; St. Albans; and Isle La-Motte, scene of Vermont's first European outpost.

The northeastern most part of Vermont is termed the "Northeast Kingdom," a nickname first applied in the 1930s. The "princes" of this sparsely settled "kingdom" are the great lumber companies who own much of the land east of Interstate 91 and north of McIndoe Falls.

Vermont's Ghosts Are Independent Too

The fiercely independent spirit of its people is among the many reasons why so many Americans love Vermont. In the best American tradition, Vermonters don't take any nonsense from outsiders. At the time of the American Revolution the other newly proclaimed states and ex-colonies weren't sure that Vermont *was* a state, as it had not been a separate colony under English rule. New Hampshire claimed lands in what is now Vermont and sold the land to settlers. New York also claimed that its northeastern boundary was the Connecticut River. Even Massachusetts made a half-hearted attempt at grabbing some of Vermont's land.

When Colonel Ethan Allen's famed Green Mountain Boys carried out the first major American offensive against the British at Fort Ticonderoga (they won easily), they already were experienced in combat—against those rascally New Yorkers. Vermont functioned as an independent republic from 1777 to 1791, when it joined the Union as the 14th state. Only three other states—Texas, California, and Hawaii—had been republics before joining the United States.

When, following the Revolution, Congress hesitated in admitting Vermont as a state, under pressure from both New York and New Hampshire, Vermont patriot Ethan Allen threatened that Vermont might consider joining Canada. That clinched it. Vermont was accepted into the union.

Vermont's first state constitution prohibited slavery—two generations before the U.S. Constitution got around to it. The good people of Vermont were so angry at Nazi aggression that the state declared war on Germany two months before the U.S. did so, following Pearl Harbor.

Vermont's ghosts, witches, and demons demonstrate the same highly independent spirit as its living population, past and present. One theory explaining why the spirits of some of the deceased remain among the living is that those spirits are not reconciled to their new existence. They simply refuse to accept death and stay in the familiar locales of their life, sometimes as benign, well-intentioned apparitions, sometimes as vengeful or possessive spirits motivated by rage at their murderers. Those robustly independent Vermonters make some very determined ghosts.

The Green Mountain state's most famous monster, "Champ," the Loch Ness–like creature said to lurk in the depths of Lake Champlain, is notably independent-minded. Evidently, Champ does not tolerate any attempts to capture, document, or photograph it and will deliberately upset the boats of anyone who ventures too close.

And so, Vermont stands tall and proud in the world of ghosts, witches, demons, monsters, and weird happenings. Characteristically, Vermont has claimed its unique place in the shadowy world of the supernatural just as it has achieved a special image as a beautiful and fascinating place in which to live or visit.

South Green Mountains

THE SOUTHERN GREEN MOUNTAINS COMPRISE ONE OF VERMONT'S
largest regions, including most of the area of the Green Mountains
National Forest. Stretching more than halfway from the southern
border with Massachusetts toward the Canadian border, the southern Green Mountains include the cities of Bennington, Rutland, and
Middlebury, together with such well-known ski resorts as Stratton
Mountain, Killington, Magic Mountain, Pico, the Mount Snow–
Haystack area, and "Suicide Six" slopes. Important historic sites
include the Bennington Battle Monument, Coolidge Homestead,
and Robert Lincoln's home.

Spirits Full of Spirits at Tunbridge World's Fair

The tiny community of Tunbridge used to host annual world's fairs,
or at least that was what Tunbridge people called their fall harvest
festival. Of course, calling a village's traditional harvest celebration
a world's fair might seem a tad boastful. Perhaps those egotistical
Tunbridgers were on to something, though, public-relations-wise.
Tunbridge's miniature world's fair was one of the handful of such
local festivals to persist through the depression years of the 1930s.

Or maybe it wasn't just the grandiose title, world's fair, that drew crowds. A unique feature of each Tunbridge world's fair was the rule that at precisely three o'clock in the afternoon, all sober persons were to be rounded up and ejected from the fair grounds. Naturally, both visitors and residents alike had to take vigorous steps to avoid the indignity of being thrown out of Tunbridge's famous world's fair. The necessary extra drink or two were downed quickly in order to qualify as a properly inebriated fair goer. After all, how would one explain being arrested for improper sobriety to one's children or grandchildren?

As a result of the rule against insufficient alcohol intake, the Tunbridge world's fair was a smashing success, full of half-smashed people. Where do the ghosts come in? As ghost hunters are well aware, manifestations of the supernatural involve auditory encounters at least as frequently as the visual variety. The local legend is that around dusk and into the early evening, the sounds of drunken laughter can be heard on the old fairgrounds—the low-lying flat meadowlands in the valley of the little river. These inebriated chuckles are most likely to be heard on October Saturday evenings, the traditional times of the fabled Tunbridge world's fair. There is no need to fear the unseen partygoers, for they are happy drunks, or at least the ghosts of happy drunks.

Drink up! You don't want to be thrown off the fairgrounds.

The Phantom "Underground Train"

It is late at night on a lonely mountain road north of Fair Haven. Four horses are laboring to draw the heavy stagecoach up a long, steep grade. Their hooves are wrapped in rags to muffle the sounds of iron horseshoes on the stony road. The brass carriage lamps on either side of the coach are not lit. The stage driver, perched high on the front of his coach, is dressed in black, matching the dull black paint of the stagecoach. Despite the fair weather, the leather curtains are drawn across the windows, and the passengers are quiet, not conversing with one another. Silence is the rule and the stakes are high, as the coach must make its way north undetected. The freedom of its passengers is at risk, for this is a "train" on the famed Underground Railroad, transporting runaway slaves to freedom in Canada.

The year could have been any time in the first sixty years of the nineteenth century, but actually, this silent passage of the mysterious darkened stagecoach is said to happen several times a year even now. This phantom coach is seen on moonless nights as though the anxious passengers and coachman are eternally reliving their dramatic dash through the night on the way to safety and freedom.

Fair Haven once was an important junction on the Underground Railroad, which was neither underground nor a railroad, but rather an organized system of transporting runaway slaves to Canada, where slavery was outlawed. A main route on the "railroad" brought the escaping slaves up Chesapeake Bay, then up the Delaware River Valley, across New Jersey to New York City, then up the Hudson Valley. A branch went through Fair Haven, then along Lake Champlain and on to Montreal.

Many Vermonters were active as "station agents" and "conductors" on the Underground Railroad. The 1777 constitutional convention of the Republic of Vermont specifically prohibited any person being held in slavery or bondage of any kind. No person was ever held in slavery in Vermont. Long before the Civil War, Vermont was so vehemently antislave that the state of Georgia once requested of President Franklin Pierce that "enough workmen be employed to dig a ditch around the state of Vermont and float it out to sea."

And so, again and again, the phantom coach crowded with fugitive slaves toils up the hills, bound for Canada. Should you glimpse it one night, silently wish them well.

The Father of Maggot Mountain

Killington Peak, at 4,241 feet above sea level, is Vermont's second highest point (Mount Mansfield tops Killington by only 154 feet). Killington is renowned as one of the largest and best ski resorts in the northeast; it is an important moneymaker in Vermont, where an old joke is that the top three favorite things to do are skiing, skiing, and skiing. Killington's ski slopes, one of which is called "the beast of the east," make the peak famous. It is the resident ghost that makes Killington a little scary in nonski season.

The ghost avoids the winter snows, for this spirit likes to see green, not white. The ghost is supposed to be that of the Reverend

Samuel Peters, who, in life, claimed to have suggested calling the state Verd-Mont, which he claimed was French for green mountains.

Actually, it was the French explorer Samuel de Champlain who, in 1609, not only gave his name to the lake he sailed, but also suggested calling the area "les Verts Mont," the green mountains. Reverend Peters claimed to have christened the state Verd-Mont in 1763 by smashing a bottle of good whiskey on the Killington Peak.

When the new state's legislature officially accepted the name "Vermont," Samuel Peters was outraged. It should be Verdmont, he insisted, as he translated Ver-Mont as "maggot mountain." *Vermis* is Latin or old French for worm and is the root of the word "vermin."

"Maggot mountain!" he would shout angrily. "They've changed my suggestion to maggot mountain." It became Peters' lifelong compulsion to revise the name to Vermont, but few listened.

The rather pompous reverend would stop strangers on the street to give them his "sermon" about mislabeling the state (and his not receiving the credit he thought due him for "christening" the state). Soon people were avoiding Reverend Peters as soon as they spotted him, and he took to running after them, shouting, "Maggot mountain—that's what they've named our beautiful state!"

Not only did Peters ignore Samuel de Champlain's application of "Les Verts Mont" to the area some 154 years before Peters "christened" the state, but the reverend was known to stretch the truth a bit, a handicap to a career in the church. Samuel Peters could be very persuasive, as he got his fellow clergymen to elect him Episcopal Bishop of Vermont in 1794. The Archbishop of Canterbury, however, refused to consecrate Peters. Maybe the Archbishop had checked up on Peters' credentials. Peters claimed to have a doctorate from the University of Cortona in Tuscany. There was no such institution.

A proven liar and conman, Samuel Peters spent the rest of his life obsessively claiming to be the true coiner of the name Verdmont, complaining that Vermont meant maggot mountain and must be changed.

Traditionally, his ghost sits atop Killington Peak in summer, sermonizing to any visitors unwary enough to come within hearing distance. "It's not maggot mountain!" the ghost shouts. "It's green mountain." It is best to avoid the ghost of the "father of maggot mountain."

Stop That Hammering!

On some nights it is hard to get to sleep in the tiny village of East Clarendon, south of Rutland. A loud hammering noise is heard, accompanied by shouts, curses, and even some laughter. But no one is to be seen. Some locals believe that Ethan Allen and his Green Mountain Boys are at it again, tearing the roof off Benjamin Spencer's house, and then putting it back on. These unseen, but very noisy, ghosts seem to be endlessly reenacting one of the funnier events in Vermont's colonial history.

What is now the proud state of Vermont once was hotly disputed territory, claimed by both the colonies of New York and New Hampshire. Blame vaguely worded deeds and boundary descriptions on the part of his arrogant and incompetent majesty, King George the Third. To make the argument worse, the "Yorkers" or local supporters of New York's claim were considered loyalists to the King, while the New Hampshire–leaning folks were determined patriots favoring independence.

The story is that the famous Revolutionary leader, Ethan Allen, accompanied by a hundred or so heavily armed patriots, decided to teach Ben Spencer a lesson. Spencer was a well-known leader of the "Yorkers" in his neighborhood. On November 21, 1773, the Green Mountain Boys put Spencer on trial right in front of his house. Spencer refused to publicly denounce King George and was judged guilty of being unpatriotic. His punishment? The patriots began tearing the roof off his house. "We'll tear down your entire house," he was warned, "unless, of course, you switch sides and become a true American."

As the patriots, fueled by a few tots of rum, gleefully ripped shingles from his roof, Benjamin Spencer experienced a change of heart. "Down with British rule! May King George descend into hell and join his cousin, the Devil!" At that, the Green Mountain Boys turned from demolition to restoration. The roof was back in place, and Ben Spencer was an enthusiastic supporter of American independence. It's amazing how persuasive the Green Mountain Boys could be when they tried. Actually, Ben Spencer was lucky. A more usual punishment for fans of King George was to see their houses torched and burned to the ground. So if you hear the sounds of hammering, but no one is there, give three cheers for America!

The Pathetic Little Ghost

There is an old tradition, now almost forgotten, of a sad little ghost in an old house in the small college town of Castleton, near Rutland. In the past, the haunted house was rented out to students at the state college in town, but few tenants stayed for long. Now the house stands empty most of the time, for many believe that it is haunted—haunted by the sad, troubled spirit of a little girl who once lived there.

Many claim to have seen the pale image of a little girl's face peering from an upstairs window. She appears to be about eight- or nine-years-old. Her expression is one of hopeless, forlorn resignation to her fate, as though she foresaw her terrible end. For the story is that she was murdered. Worse than that, she almost certainly had been shamefully abused before her death, probably at the hands of an uncle.

During their (usually) brief occupancy of the haunted house, many college students experienced hearing a child's whimpering cry coming from the upstairs hall near the top of the stairs. This low, moaning cry was accompanied by the sound of a body tumbling down the stairs. Local people say that the little girl whose spirit supposedly lingers in the house died of a broken neck, having been pushed down the stairs. The circumstances of the fall always were shrouded in mystery. An agonizingly unhappy childhood, cut short by a mysterious fall down the stairs might account for her unhappy spirit's presence in the house.

The most unnerving manifestations of the sad little ghost are the tap on the shoulder and the whispered plea for help, both of which had been experienced by college student tenants over the years. While sitting up late reading, the person allegedly feels a gentle tap on the shoulder. On looking around, there is no one there. The bedsprings creak and the mattress shifts, as though a weight had been added; then a hot breath in the person's ear would be accompanied by a childish, whispered plea, "Help me! Please help me!" But, of course, there was no one there. No wonder that most temporary occupants of this house left after a few weeks or even a few nights. Will the troubled girl's spirit ever find peace?

Chasing a Ghost

The young family had just moved into an apartment in Rutland when the trouble started. The young couple and their three-year-old son were newcomers to Vermont, looking forward to a fresh start in the beautiful Green Mountains. Their apartment was the second floor of an old Victorian-style house on a quiet side street. The rent was quite attractive, but the price was low for a reason, as they soon discovered.

They had decided to use the smaller of the two bedrooms for their little son, but he seemed to have some difficulty in falling asleep. The large window in his room rattled noisily, as though a strong wind was shaking it in its frame. The young couple figured that strong winds probably were not unusual in these mountains, and thought little of it at first. But then they began to notice that from whatever direction the wind blew, the window rattled and shook. In fact, the window seemed to shudder even on calm evenings. What was going on?

Their toddler, Tommy, eventually got used to his noisy window, but he seemed uneasy on a few occasions. It seems that the racket from the window was being supplemented by unexplained pounding noises on the solid oak floors. It sounded like loud, hesitant footsteps, as though a very heavy person were moving slowly across the floor. Now things were getting serious.

The noise level was escalating and so was the fear level in the family. Finally, a truly frightening event sent them in search of help. A heavy old table, left behind by a former tenant, stood in little Tommy's room. Late one night, the couple were awakened by Tommy's terrified cries, accompanied by a loud stomping sound. When the husband and wife entered their son's room, they saw that one of the heavy table legs had been unbolted from the table and lay in the opposite corner of the room.

Their son could not possibly have detached the table leg and moved it by himself. Was the table leg the cause of the heavy footstep sounds?

The husband's mother, a deeply religious person, suggested they consult a priest, despite objections from her nonbelieving daughter-in-law. It had always bothered the mother that her grandson had never been baptized, nor for that matter had his mother.

When a local priest was asked to perform an exorcism, he had to refuse. He was not authorized to perform one, he explained, and exorcism was a very rarely used rite of the church. He advised that instead of a formal exorcism he would visit the apartment and bless it with holy water, and that both mother and son should be baptized.

This was done. A large cross was hung on the wall by Tommy's bed, and the young mother began wearing a gold cross on a chain about her neck, a gift from her mother-in-law. Thankfully, there have been no more mysterious noises in the child's room or anywhere else. The young family has become regular churchgoers as well.

The Prankster Ghost at the Equinox

The Equinox Resort and Spa in Manchester is one of Vermont's oldest, most famous, and most prestigious hotels. In operation since 1769, it started as a country tavern where patriots plotted revolutionary actions over a few brews. The Equinox evolved into one of New England's most fashionable resorts in the nineteenth century, attracting the rich and famous to the picturesque little town of which it is the crown jewel.

Placed on the national register of historic places in 1972, the Equinox has been resurrected as Vermont's most luxurious resort, providing its guests with the finest in accommodations, food, entertainment, and ghosts. In keeping with its reputation, the ghosts of the Equinox include those of the highest social rank and claim to fame: None other than the spirits of Mary Todd Lincoln and the presidential couple's youngest son, Thomas "Tad," are among the many ghosts encountered at the fabled majestic old hotel.

It is said that, on occasion, the sounds of a sobbing child can be heard, accompanied by a mother's comforting voice, on the third floor. Some believe these ghosts to be those of Mrs. Lincoln and her son Tad. Mary Lincoln was a frequent guest at the Equinox. It was her refuge from the humid heat of Washington summers and the tensions of the wartime White House. Mrs. Lincoln was so fond of the tranquil and luxurious Equinox, in fact, that she planned an extended vacation there with her husband in the summer of 1865 to help the president recover from the terrible strain of the Civil War. But that was not to be, as President Lincoln died from the assassin's bullet early in the morning of April 15, 1865.

In the summer of 1862, Mary and Tad Lincoln arrived at the Equinox to gain a respite from mourning the death of William "Willie," the president's favorite son and Tad's closest brother, both in age and in temperament. Both Tad and Willie had been stricken with typhoid fever that previous winter, but Willie had died while Tad recovered. Tad now had a classic case of survivor's guilt—why had he been spared and his brother taken?

Willie and Tad had been known, affectionately, as the "tyrants of the White House" for their rambunctious sense of fun. They once organized a circus, featuring their menagerie of pets, on the White House roof, insisting that the entire staff as well as visitors attend performances. Tad once hitched his pet goat to a toy wagon and caused chaos at an official reception. The two irrepressible brothers had taken on themselves the job of lightening the somber pressures of the wartime White House.

Now only Tad was left. He threw himself into the role of family clown. Making his father laugh became his goal. At the Equinox, when Tad and his mother were joined by elder brother Robert Lincoln, then a student at Harvard, Tad continued his playful pranks. A favorite was to sneak up behind a dignified adult, tap the person on the shoulder, and then race away.

Although Tad died in 1875 at the age of eighteen, visitors to the Equinox ever since have felt gentle taps on the back but, turning, see no one. Is the ghost of Tad Lincoln still playing his tricks?

The Ghost in Tennis Whites

A seemingly out-of-place spirit is said to appear from time to time in the tiny village of Plymouth Notch. It is the phantom of a teenaged boy dressed in "tennis whites"—shirt, shorts, socks, and shoes. The boy is limping noticeably. Who else could this ghost be but Calvin Coolidge Jr., younger son of the thirtieth president of the United States?

Everything about the village, now frozen in time exactly as it looked on August 3, 1923, is connected with the Coolidge family. On that date, Vice President Calvin Coolidge was sworn into office as the new president following the death of President Warren Harding. The oath of office was administered by the light of a kerosene lamp by the new president's father, a notary public and former sheriff.

The village was the boyhood home of the new president who had been born across the street in the building that contained the general store. The entire village has been donated to the state as a historic park by the president's older son, successful businessman and conservationist John Coolidge.

But why would the spirit of the younger son still appear in Plymouth Notch, and why is he in tennis clothes and limping? It is a sad story, and one that caused a president to decide against running for reelection.

As in many families, the elder son was the heir to the father's driving ambition to do good and to do well. John was the serious, determined, and dedicated image of his father, while Cal Junior was more lighthearted, playful, and outgoing. Young Cal was a charmer in contrast to his notoriously tight-lipped father.

In common with many other presidential children, President Coolidge's sons found the constant company of their secret service protectors to be a little annoying sometimes, and didn't welcome the overbearing attention of crowds in public places. Thus, the family's frequent visits to remote Plymouth Notch represented relative freedom and quality time with doting relatives.

In the White House, with both parents absorbed in official duties and older brother away at university, young Cal's retreat was the tennis court on the south lawn. He would play game after game until he was exhausted. During the summer of 1924, Cal Junior developed a blister on his toe while playing tennis, but kept right on playing several more matches. Within hours, septicemia had set in. In the days before antibiotics, blood poisoning overcame him. He died on July 7. His father was stunned. All the privileges and powers of the presidency could not help him save his son. The president later wrote, "He begged me to help him, but I could not. When he went, all the power and glory of the presidency went with him." President Coolidge refused to run for reelection and returned to Plymouth Notch.

And so, Cal Junior, still in his tennis whites, limps through the single street and surrounding fields of Plymouth Notch, remembering the good times. He is, in his father's words, "a boy for all eternity."

The Ghost Who Witnessed History

The distinguished looking bearded gentleman, immaculately dressed in a business suit, waistcoat, and tie, paces the front terrace of an impressive Georgian revival mansion just south of Manchester. Or, rather, his ghost walks there, for Robert Todd Lincoln, the only son of Abraham Lincoln to live to maturity, died on July 25, 1926.

Robert Lincoln's ghost wears a rather melancholy, reflective face, as did the few photographs for which he posed during his adult life. He had much to be sad about, despite having achieved great success as a business executive, diplomat, and high-ranking government official.

Why would the ghost of President Lincoln's eldest son appear at this splendid house overlooking the Green Mountains? Robert Lincoln loved the Vermont countryside more than any other place. He built "Hildene," his twenty-three-room mansion, as a summer home, which became his retirement home. He died at Hildene (old English for "hills and valleys") and was buried there briefly before his body was moved to Arlington National Cemetery as he requested in his will.

In addition to the tragedy of his father's brutal assassination, Robert had to cope with the deaths of his three younger brothers: Edward at age three, William at age ten, and Thomas "Tad" at age eighteen. He was compelled, as well, to place his mother, Mary Todd Lincoln, in a mental institution when she began wandering the streets, trying to sell her clothing under the unfounded delusion that she had no money. Also, Robert's only son, Abraham Lincoln II, died at age seventeen.

In personal accomplishments, Robert was an outstanding success. Following his graduation from Harvard, he joined General Grant's personal staff and witnessed Lee's surrender at Appomattox Court House. Invited to attend the theater with his parents on the evening of Friday, April 14, 1865, Robert declined and stayed in the White House due to exhaustion. He raced to his stricken father's bedside on hearing of the shooting at Ford's Theater and afterward lamented not being present to foil John Wilkes Booth.

In a spooky chain of events, Robert Lincoln was present when both Presidents Garfield and McKinley were shot. Robert was

Garfield's Secretary of War and was an arm's length away when Garfield was shot in a Washington train station. President McKinley had invited Robert Lincoln to join him at the Pan American Exposition in Buffalo, where, again, Robert was only a few feet away when the assassin fired a bullet into the president.

After serving as President Benjamin Harrison's minister to Great Britain, Robert embarked on a career in business, becoming president of the Pullman Company, a leading corporation of the day. He also helped organize AT&T and the Chicago Commonwealth Edison. Republican party leaders tried several times to get him to run for the White House, but Robert Lincoln refused. He said that the politicians didn't want Robert Todd Lincoln to run, they wanted Abraham Lincoln's son to run.

He believed that his father had much preferred Willie and Tad over him. His father even admitted that there was friction between father and eldest son, because, he said, "Robert is so much like me." Robert resented being able to see his father in the White House by appointment only, for ten minutes at a time, though the President would spend hours with his younger sons, even allowing Willie and Tad to interrupt cabinet meetings.

The three presidential assassinations traumatized him, so that he began to fear being with the president in public. Was he some sort of magnet for assassins? He chose to be buried in Arlington National Cemetery, his right as a former soldier, rather than join his parents and brothers in Springfield, Illinois. He had had enough association with murdered presidents.

In one final irony, the body of John Kennedy, the fourth victim of a presidential assassin, came to be buried about seventy yards from the grave of Robert Todd Lincoln. No wonder that Robert's spirit has chosen to haunt Hildene rather than the White House, Arlington, or Springfield.

The Ghostly Sentries of Bennington Monument

Geography always has been an important consideration in military strategy and operations. From ancient times to the present, control of the heights has been an objective of commanders. A good lookout position, as atop a hill, can deny the enemy the advantage of surprise in event of an attack.

For these reasons, the ghosts of those American soldiers who fell in the Battle of Bennington apparently have decided to use the great monument as a lookout tower. Still the tallest structure in Vermont, the 306-foot granite shaft once was the tallest battle monument in the world. By day, tourists can see three states—Vermont, New York, and Massachusetts, for the monument stands at the summit of a broad hill.

By night, or so it is said, ghostly sentries keep a close watch for the campfires of the enemy—that is, the British. The Battle of Bennington was a crushing blow to the British during the American Revolution, and one of the few cases in which an improvised, ragtag army of untrained volunteers decisively beat a professional force.

British General Burgoyne was running low on supplies and heard about a hilltop storehouse in Bennington guarded only by a handful of untrained American militia. Easy pickings, he thought, sending an army led by Hessian Colonel Baum to seize the supplies. But the Americans were watching. American General John Stark, who had seen battle under George Washington at Trenton and Princeton, two key American victories, was ready.

Out of total British and Hessian forces of about 1,350, Stark's men killed over 200 and took 600 prisoners. American casualties were thirty dead and forty wounded. American morale got a big boost and the lesson was learned—keep a close watch on the enemy's movements.

Within the hollow granite shaft, 412 steps zigzag past thirty-four landings to the lookout windows. Tourists can take an elevator up the shaft, and the steps have been sealed off since 1975. Only security, maintenance, and phantom soldiers have access to the steps now.

Many report seeing the faint glow of candle lanterns at the lookout windows late at night. Watchmen report hearing footsteps on the sealed-off stairs after the 5 p.m. closing. Are the spirits of Revolutionary War American soldiers still on sentry duty, taking advantage of the monument's height to watch for the return of the British?

The Perennial Séance

This much is historical fact. Millionaire John Bowman built a mansion in Cuttingsville, some ten miles southeast of Rutland, in 1880. He also had built, across the road in a corner of a cemetery, an elaborate, Egyptian-style granite mausoleum. It is also true that Mr. Bowman had a life-sized marble statue carved of himself, kneeling on the steps of his family tomb, holding a funeral wreath and a key. For ten years, John Bowman lived in his mansion, looking across the road at the mausoleum with the kneeling statue of himself on its steps. Finally, in death he took his place inside the mausoleum.

Why was he so morbidly focused on death? Both daughters died in childhood, followed by his wife, just as the plans for their Vermont retirement home were finished. This was a time in popular culture when there was a great deal of interest in spiritualism and mediums.

Bowman began inviting well-known mediums to hold nightly séances in his home. The servants would hear various rappings, moans, and distorted voices during these late evening sessions. No one will ever know what degree of success the mediums may have had in contacting John Bowman's wife and daughters. It does appear that Bowman derived some peace of mind from these spiritualist sessions, and it is certain that the mediums helped lighten his wallet.

A fervent believer in physical reincarnation, Bowman's will left a fund of money to maintain his home exactly as he left it. His will further stipulated that his servants prepare an evening meal and place it in the dining room each night. Evidently John Bowman expected to return to his home and eat dinner, at least in spirit.

While the nightly repasts never were eaten, the servants did report that mysterious sounds and lights behind closed doors made it seem that the nightly séances had continued. The really weird part of the story is the report that, for several hours, each evening, the kneeling statue of John Bowman on the steps of the family mausoleum disappeared, afterward resuming his place. Did the spirit of John somehow inhabit his own statue? To this day, it is said that the locals avoid going anywhere near the Bowman house or the Bowman mausoleum after dark.

The Ghost of the Little Giant

There have been two Vermont-born presidents—Chester A. Arthur and Calvin Coolidge. Both men had been vice presidents, promoted to the White House by the deaths of their predecessors. A third native Vermonter made a determined, desperate effort to become president, but lost.

Stephen Douglas was born on April 23, 1813, to a college-educated physician father in Brandon, Vermont. His father died soon after his birth, leaving little Stephen in the care of a grandfather with a strong interest in politics. Stephen later moved to Illinois, where, as a "Jacksonian Democrat," he was elected to the state legislature at the same time as another ambitious young lawyer, Abraham Lincoln.

Stephen soon earned a reputation as a dynamic, persuasive speaker full of energy. One contemporary called him a "steam engine in breeches," but the nickname that stuck with him for life was "the little giant," for he was only five feet, four inches tall.

It was in a campaign for the U.S. Senate in 1858 that Douglas, and his opponent, Abraham Lincoln, had a series of seven three-hour-long debates that brought both men national recognition. Douglas believed that the Union was a confederation of sovereign states—states that should choose for themselves on the burning issue of slavery. Although personally opposed to slavery, Douglas had married a wealthy southern woman who owned 100 slaves. Stephen earned 20 percent of the plantation's profits as business manager.

On key, nonslavery issues, Douglas agreed with Lincoln, advocating building a transcontinental railroad and granting free land to settlers in the west. Douglas' argument that each state should decide for itself, whether it was a free state or a slave state, actually cost him votes in the south. When the Democratic National Convention nominated Douglas for president, the Southern Democrats broke away and nominated President Buchanan's vice president, John Breckenridge, as their candidate.

Convinced that only compromise could save the Union, Stephen Douglas campaigned ceaselessly, frantically trying to avoid the coming conflict. He was bitterly disappointed by Lincoln's victory. To his credit, however, when Fort Sumter was fired upon, Douglas pledged his full support to Lincoln.

Less than two months after the start of the Civil War that Stephen Douglas had hoped to forestall, he died of complete exhaustion and, his friends believed, a broken heart. It is not surprising that his spirit should return to his birthplace roots where he first absorbed his principles of fiercely defending each state's right to choose its own destiny.

And so, the diminutive, cocky phantom of "the little giant" strides purposefully about the little village of Brandon. Ironically, Abraham Lincoln's son and granddaughter died at Robert Lincoln's estate, "Hildene," less than fifty miles away.

Ghosts of the Royalton Raid

One of the ugliest incidents of the American Revolution took place in Royalton and nearby Tunbridge in October of 1780. The Royalton Raid, carried out by some 300 Indians under the command of a British Lieutenant, John Horton, was designed to terrify and demoralize patriotic Vermonters. That it did, very successfully, and the horror is revisited every October according to those who have witnessed the ghosts of the raiders and their victims.

It is a moonless night toward the close of Vermont's glorious "leaf season." The brilliant crimson leaves of sugar maples are falling from the trees, forming drifts of vivid color on the ground. A wonderful time to be in Vermont, except during the American Revolution, when Vermont's accessibility from Canada meant the ever-present possibility of raids. The Royalton Raid was particularly vicious. The British convinced their Indian allies to attack American farms and settlements. Supplied with British guns and, some say, whiskey and rum as fringe benefits, the Indians eagerly anticipated looting American homes and stores. An added attraction, conveniently ignored by the hypocritical British, was a chance to obtain slaves. It was a long-standing Indian custom for them to take home prisoners of war as slaves.

One by one, outlying farms came under attack. Men who offered resistance were cut down by rifle fire or tomahawks. Women and children were roped together and marched off into slavery. Some never returned. Others eventually were set free in Canada and found their way home again. Horses were stolen for the use of the raiders. Cattle, sheep, and pigs were slaughtered and left to rot in the fields. Houses and barns were torched.

To this day, it is said, if you listen carefully in the dead of an October night, you can hear the cries and moans of the white prisoners, forced to march by their Indian captors. One ghost stands out among the others, that of a courageous farm wife who defied her assailants, fighting so valiantly that she earned the respect of the marauding warriors. The pugnacious ghost is said to be that of Hannah Handy. Dragged from her house and knocked to the ground with a blow from a gun butt, Hannah staggered after the raiders and succeeded in snatching nine white children from their Indian guards. Out of admiration and respect for her perseverance and courage, the Indians let her go home with the little troop of rescued children.

So listen carefully for the ghosts of the Royalton Raid. You might hear an echo of American history.

The Enchanted Stone of Glastenbury

Glastenbury Mountain, at 3,748 feet above sea level, is not particularly high for Vermont. The whole state averages 1,000 feet in elevation, and there are twenty-one peaks higher than 3,500 feet. But there is something special and mysterious about Glastenbury Mountain.

The popular Appalachian Trail, a favorite of hikers from Maine to Georgia, passes close by Glastenbury Mountain. At least a dozen hikers have disappeared while hiking in the vicinity. Police in the area even have speculated about the possibility of a serial killer operating in this section of the Green Mountain National Forest.

An old American Indian legend concerning Glastenbury offers a possible supernatural explanation that is even scarier than a serial killer. The Abnaki Indians feared Glastenbury peak and stayed well clear of it. The strong winds around the mountain, changing direction frequently and unpredictably, were thought to be the messengers of evil and death. The Abnaki cautioned European pioneers not to settle in the vicinity of Glastenbury Mountain, but they did anyway. The forty-square mile town of Glastenbury never really prospered, however. Once entitled to send a representative to the state legislature, Glastenbury town has dwindled to seven inhabi-

tants, only three of whom could vote, when the state dissolved the town as a political unit in 1937. Glastenbury had become a ghost town in several meanings of the phrase: The mountain and its namesake town always had been haunted, claimed the Indians.

An Abnaki legend says that there is an enchanted stone somewhere on the slopes of Glastenbury Mountain. This huge stone, if stepped on, will open and swallow a person, instantly returning to its deceptively normal appearance. One moment you're there, the next you are gone without a trace. The victims of the enchanted stone don't even have time to scream, it is said.

Which is the true explanation for the mysterious disappearances around Glastenbury Mountain—the enchanted stone that swallow people whole, or the vicious serial killer that some suspect? It is a tough choice as to which is the more horrific.

In the Lyon's Den

As Vermonters would be the first to admit, and even boast, Vermont politicians are a cantankerous lot on occasion. Certainly as a group they have achieved a collective reputation as being highly individualistic and, perhaps, a tad pugnacious. Vermont's elected officials often buck national trends.

The little town of Fair Haven, near the New York border, is said to host the ghost of its famous son, Matthew Lyon. Matthew was described by some contemporaries as being brilliant, headstrong, pugnacious, and Irish—a not uncommon combination. Born in Ireland in 1750, he arrived in Vermont in 1783 and immediately went into politics. He was well-connected politically. His first wife was a niece of Ethan Allen. His second wife was the daughter of Vermont's first governor, Thomas Chittenden.

Lyon served several terms in the state legislature before being sent to Congress in 1797. He was an outspoken critic of President John Adams and the Federalists, but did not take criticism well himself. When insulted by a Connecticut congressman, Lyon spat in his face right on the floor of the House. Lyon's criticism of President Adams, published in his own newspaper in an article called "The Scourge of Aristocracy and Repository of Important Political Truth," landed him in jail, charged with treason under the highly controversial Sedition Act. He spent four months in Vergennes jail, during which time he was reelected to Congress by an overwhelming majority. Matthew Lyons came to be known as "the man who elected Jefferson." When the House of Representatives had to vote to break a tie between presidential candidates Aaron Burr and Thomas Jefferson, Lyon cast the deciding vote for Jefferson, his hero.

In addition to his political career and publishing his newspaper, Matthew built and operated a tavern on Main Street in Fair Haven, the location of which is said to be haunted by his ghost. His ghost is said to appear more frequently whenever any politicians attempt to quell criticism by labeling it treason. Matthew Lyon, dead or alive, simply won't tolerate any attempts at limiting debate or stifling criticism of presidents.

The Bewitched Covered Bridge

Vermont's covered bridges, and there are many of them, are among its most picturesque tourist attractions. Several are known to be haunted. Stowe's Gold Brook Bridge, also called Stone Hollow Bridge, is said to have a resident ghost, for example. One of the state's longest covered bridges, the Scott Bridge at Townshend (three spans totaling 276 feet), was also the first to be marked for preservation. Maybe no one was brave enough to suggest its demolition, for the Scott Bridge is said to be bewitched or haunted.

One of the bridge's spans is 166 feet, an engineering triumph in the days of wooden bridges. Scott Bridge may be one of the most famous, and photographed, sites in Vermont. A funny thing about many, though not all, of these photos is that a blurry or foggy shadow appears on the bridge that was not there, or noticed, when the picture was taken. Fuzzy photos are not the only oddity about Scott Bridge. In the days of horse-drawn vehicles crossing the bridge, locals learned to avoid the bridge on nights of a full moon. At such times, a night crossing became a horrific experience. In mid-span, horses would scream, rear up, and suddenly run for their lives. Later examination would show deep gashes on the backs and flanks of the poor horses, together with long scratches along the sides of wagons and carriages. When cars replaced horses, full moonlit transits of Scott Bridge produced mysterious gouges and scrapes on the car bodies, as though some powerful and aggressive predator were attacking passing vehicles.

According to a legend, in the 1870s a tragedy occurred on Scott Bridge. A young housemaid, an Irish immigrant, fell in love with her employer's son and became pregnant. She and her lover agreed to run away and get married, starting a new life together away from his snobbish disapproving family. They were to rendezvous at Scott Bridge. She waited most of the night, but he never showed up. Alone, abandoned, miserable, and hopeless, she hanged herself from the bridge's rafters so that her body would block traffic until decently cared for.

Her mistlike phantom is said to still pace the bridge, waiting in vain for her faithless lover. Some psychics claim that the bridge has become a portal, or gateway, to hell and must be avoided on nights of a full moon. Probably good advice.

The Most Flamboyant Ghost

The stout, middle-aged gentleman is dressed in mid-Victorian finery, with a colorful silk tie, embroidered vest, black tophat, gleaming polished shoes, and carrying a gold-tipped ebony cane. Diamonds blaze from his tie stickpin and his many rings. A heavy gold watch chain stretches across his ample stomach. Everything about him seems to shout, "Money! Success! Fame!" This gaudy ghost, for he isn't really there in the flesh, strolls pompously about the little town of Pownal, where he was born on April 1, 1834.

Those who've encountered Vermont's most flamboyant ghost believe they've seen Vermont's least typical son, James "Jubilee Jim" Fisk. Jim Fisk in life was pretty much the exact opposite of the popular image of Vermonters, who are supposed to be salt-of-the-earth types—unassuming, modest, practical, fiercely independent, yet cooperative and community-minded, and, of course, shrewd. Jim Fisk got the shrewd part down alright, but he also was boastful, self-absorbed, ostentatious, greedy, and really, really flamboyant. He also was an extrovert with a great deal of charm and a good sense of humor. In his time, the public were entertained and amused by his antics, and willing to forgive much of his bad behavior because of his charm.

Jim Fisk was among the most colorful characters of the "robber baron" wheelers and dealers of what Mark Twain labeled "The Gilded Age." He was born the son of a country peddler, the prototype of the "Yankee trader." Traveling about with their wagon of goods—a kind of mobile general store—these merchants were famous for driving a good bargain, sometimes bordering on fraud for the unwary.

Young Jim had an expert teacher and role model in the art of making a deal. He soon bought out his dad, and at one time had five gaudily painted wagons carrying his wares to country folk across the state. Then he discovered Wall Street, which he regarded as a kind of crooked casino where ruthless operators could score millions in stock scams. His manipulation of Erie Railroad stock became the classic fraud and made him a national figure. Ordinary Americans forgave his getting rich on questionable stock deals, because they didn't buy stocks anyhow, and those who speculated in securities were seldom honest, in the popular view.

Jim had a series of equally colorful mistresses. His last paramour fancied herself an opera star, so Jim bought her an opera house of her own. This outraged another lover of hers, who shot Jim Fisk dead, at the age of thirty-seven. At least he shot Jim in the lobby of New York's grandest hotel, so that he could die in the splendor he so admired. No doubt, the ghost of Jim Fisk wanted to hang out far from Wall Street, in a little Vermont town where he would stand out from the crowd. Never fear meeting his ghost, for he merely will smile, tip his hat to the females of the species, and then gracefully disappear before his ghostly presence can cause alarm.

A Ghostly Quarrel

Bennington's Old Burying Ground on Monument Avenue is a tourist attraction second only to the town's battle monument. Located next to the First Congregational Church, said by many to be the most beautiful church in Vermont, the Old Burying Ground's chief claim to fame rests upon its most illustrious tenants—the earthly remains of six governors of Vermont, many of the state's "founding fathers," and of one of America's best known twentieth-century poets, Robert Frost. Frost's tombstone bears the epitaph "I had a lover's quarrel with the world."

But a different kind of quarrel rages among the ghosts of those buried here, for they include the spirits of soldiers from both sides of the Battle of Bennington. The ghosts of the British and American soldiers can be heard arguing, it is said, late at night and into the early hours of the morning. Dawn apparently ends this continuing debate until well after the next nightfall. Adding to the confusion of many hoarse whispers rising from the graves is the fact that the British side of the argument often is supported by ghostly phrases in German. Many on the British side were, in fact, Hessian mercenaries under the command of Colonel Baum, who also was killed in the ill-fated offensive of the British-Hessian forces.

Soldiers being soldiers, even those given proper Christian burial in a churchyard, a certain amount of profanity tends to enter these spirited discussions of politics and military strategy. Those brave enough to visit the Old Burying Ground around midnight report a most unnerving experience. Whenever the soldier ghosts utter curses, which happens fairly often, the carved stone angels atop some gravestones turn, frowning, toward the source of the offending language. Even ghostly soldiers in the heat of argument take notice at this. There is no record of what the other permanent residents of the Old Burying Ground make of this. It might be a good idea to avoid the graveyard after dark, but if you must go, don't voice an opinion about the Battle of Bennington.

Breathing Room

There is a house in North Bennington that contained, at least briefly, a most helpful and compassionate ghost. It is a very ordinary looking suburban house built in the 1960s, proof that not all haunted houses must look like gothic castles or dilapidated Victorian monstrosities.

This particular modest, unremarkable house harbored a spirit who actually saved a young boy's life. The first owner of the house and lifelong resident suffered from emphysema. This chronic lung disease develops slowly but causes irreversible damage to the patient's lungs. Gradually, emphysema causes shortness of breath, weakness, lethargy, and weight loss. Eventually, the patient slips into an increasingly deep coma, leading to death. It is a long, agonizing ordeal, not only for the victim, but for family caretakers as well.

As anyone who has had occasion to struggle for a breath knows, even a very brief time without adequate fresh air can be terrifying and panicking. The slowly dying old man (we'll call him Tom Snow) repeatedly begged his wife and family to pray for him, which they did fervently. Their most heartfelt prayers, of course, could not halt the progress of the disease. Tom finally died and was buried nearby.

After Tom's death his widow began to hear a ghostly struggle for breath in his bedroom late at night. The labored breathing, the painful gasps for air that had become so familiar to her during her husband's long decline could still be heard! What to do?

Tom's widow consulted a psychic, who, after visiting the house, had two pieces of advice: try to persuade the spirit, being dead, that it now could breathe normally, and get out of the house. The widow did both.

The next occupants of the house were a young family whose toddler, Mason, had severe allergies and frequent bronchitis. Many a night poor little Mason slept sitting up in bed, a vaporizer at his side, struggling to breathe. His worried parents kept waking up to check on their little son and noticed something odd. There seemed to be a faint sound of deep, relaxed breathing in their own bedroom. It was as though someone unseen was enjoying a natural, steady and dreamless sleep. When they learned the history of the house from neighbors, about poor Tom Snow, they decided to move little Mason into the "breathing room." Perhaps the slow, steady cadence of deep, untroubled breaths would lull Mason to sleep.

It worked. Their toddler, now sleeping in the "breathing room," surrounded by the reassuring sounds of normal rhythm of sleep, began to sleep and breathe normally himself. It was as though Mason's breathing became synchronized with the room's faint ghostly respiration. Had the ghost of old Tom Snow come back to somehow aid a fellow lung disease victim?

All Mason's parents know is that their child recovered from his breathing difficulties and the room itself became very quiet. Perhaps the ghost of the "breathing room" found peace at last in relieving the suffering of an innocent child.

North
Green Mountains

THIS LARGE REGION CONTAINS AMERICA'S SMALLEST AND ONE OF ITS most picturesque state capitals, Montpelier. The world-famous granite quarrying center of Barre has become a tourist attraction, along with important ski resorts like Stowe, Smuggler's Notch, Jay Peak, and Mad River Glen. This rugged region also contains Vermont's highest peak, Mount Mansfield.

The Admiral Salutes the Flag

They say it only happens at the early morning flag-raising ceremonies at Vermont's state capitol building, and only on certain dates with patriotic significance. The proudly erect figure, dressed in the dark blue and gold uniform of a United States admiral, stands briefly at the foot of the capitol grounds, salutes Old Glory as it is raised over the stately building, and then simply fades from sight once the flag has reached the top of its staff.

The phantom admiral is said to appear on Memorial Day, the 4th of July, President's Day, and, of course, April 30th. Why April 30th? Because the ghost is that of Admiral George Dewey and the date is the anniversary of his greatest triumph, and claim to fame, the Battle of Manilla Bay on April 30, 1898.

George Dewey was born in the shadow of Vermont's statehouse; his birthplace, since moved a few blocks west of the capitol on State

Street, still stands. His victory over the Spanish fleet during the Spanish-American War made him a national hero. He is a special hero to his fellow Vermonters, for he personified the best characteristics of the citizens of the Green Mountain State. George was fiercely independent, boldly decisive, and inclined to ignore the minutia, but not the spirit, of the rules. Even his fellow Vermonters might have described him as a "tad ornery." For example, in his freshman year at Annapolis, George set some kind of record by receiving 113 demerits. He did, however, graduate fifth in his class and went on to a distinguished career. He served with Admiral Farragut's fleet in the capture of New Orleans during the Civil War. When the Spanish-American War broke out, then Assistant Secretary of the Navy Theodore Roosevelt bypassed seven higher-ranking officers to give Dewey command of the Asiatic squadron consisting of five cruisers and one gunboat, then based at Hong Kong. Roosevelt admired Dewey's willingness to run risks without undue deference to the rules, a trait that Teddy Roosevelt happened to share. Admiral Dewey's bold leadership at the Battle of Manilla Bay resulted in the disabling and sinking of the entire Spanish fleet and the silencing of Spanish shore batteries. Total American casualties in that victory? Zero. No wonder a small smile can be seen beneath the elegant mustache on the ghost's face as he salutes the flag he served so well. Long live the spirit of Admiral George Dewey, a great American and a great Vermonter.

The Ghost Who Chases Snowflakes

While ghost appearances are not exactly rare in Vermont, or anywhere else for that matter, a ghost at Jerico behaves in a most unusual manner. Folks in this small town east of Burlington have observed the figure of a stooped, elderly man carrying a small board covered in black velvet. He seldom strays more than a few feet outside his specially constructed studio, and this apparition is seen only on snowy days.

Local folks who've encountered the ghost have observed it exposing the black velvet board to the swirling snowflakes in winter, then quickly ducking back into the studio with his prize—a sample of the snowflakes that fall in such abundance on Vermont every winter. The ghost is dressed warmly in overcoat, scarf, gloves, and hat, for the inside of his little studio is at least as cold as the outdoors. The studio is refrigerated to preserve the snowflakes until they can be recorded on film through a micro-photography process invented by the photographer.

The ghost is that of a W. A. Bentley, an eccentric photographer and scientist whose lifelong passion was the study of snowflakes. Every winter for decades, Bentley would wait patiently for snow to begin falling. Out would come his "cold board"—a thin board of wood covered in black velvet on which he would catch more specimens for the camera. Bentley took over 5,300 exquisitely detailed micro-photographs of snowflakes—the largest collection of its kind in the world.

Bentley's ghost never interacts with the living. This ghost ignores any person who might happen to see it, as Bentley in death, as in life, focuses on his capture of the unique and fragile crystals that so fascinated him. The apparition is seen only briefly before it disappears back into the ice-cold studio to make yet another image for his vast collection.

Of course, the ghostly form, appearing only during snowstorms, might just be a trick of light and shadow amid the swirling flakes. What a good thing that Bentley was born in Vermont instead of, say, Florida.

The Legend of Hell's Half Acre

Near the tiny town of Bristol, east of Vergennes, is a weird site known as "Hell's Half Acre." It just looks like a place where no one would want to linger—a place of no value to a would-be farmer or settler. Huge boulders lay tumbled about a rocky bed that bears little soil. A maze of cracks have split rocks into many crevasses and little caves. Tall trees provide a dense shade so that the atmosphere is one of gloomy solitude.

Geologists explain Hell's Half Acre as a relic of the great sheet of ice that once descended on New England, bringing gigantic rocks from as far away as Canada and dumping them in jumbled piles here and there as the ice finally melted away. Local people have another explanation, however. This foreboding area, they say, was cursed by the devil himself and is best avoided, especially at night.

Hell's Half Acre, however, has been the object of repeated treasure hunts by both the living and the dead. Men and ghosts alike have been drawn to this rocky wilderness by stories of a fabulous treasure buried here. Hell's Half Acre literally is honeycombed with holes and trenches dug in a so-far futile effort to find the lost treasure supposedly buried here.

There are several versions of the story of DeGrau's treasure. One is that a mysterious stranger named DeGrau, said to have been a Spaniard, was discovered prowling about Hell's Half Acre by curious locals. He told a fantastic story. His father, a miner by trade, had stumbled upon a rich vein of silver while investigating the geologic curiosities of the area. He returned with a small band of miners and opened a mine in secret. His mine yielded an immense hoard of silver, which DeGrau hid in a cave, planning to return with enough wagons to carry the fortune back to civilization. DeGrau treacherously killed his associates one night, burying their bloody remains atop the treasure. The silver would be his, and his alone.

But he never returned. He died of fever, but not before drawing a treasure map to guide his son to the silver hoard. Young DeGrau, frustrated in his many attempts to retrieve his inheritance, offered to share the silver with local men who would help search Hell's Half Acre. Many empty holes soon pockmarked the neighborhood, but not one ounce of silver was ever found.

Stories began to spread that no one could ever unearth the treasure because it was cursed by the spirits of the miners so callously slain by the elder DeGrau. These ghosts, it is claimed, are determined to keep the treasure for themselves. And so the spirits move the treasure to a new hiding place every night. Mysterious flickering lights can be seen late at night in Hell's Half Acre as the ghosts protect their silver from the living by repeatedly digging it up and reburying it elsewhere among the rocks and caves.

The treasure has never been found, which may be just as well, considering its ghostly guardians. So stay away from Hell's Half Acre, especially after dark.

The Ghost of Bristol Bill

The tiny village of Groton, east of Barre, is said to be the hangout of a very aggressive ghost—the shade of the famous outlaw called Bristol Bill. Bristol Bill was the mid-nineteenth century equivalent of John Dillinger, the famous bank robber of the 1930s. Like

Dillinger, Bristol Bill had a flair for the dramatic. He became famous on two continents as a bank robber and counterfeiter, and he finally was captured in a lumberjack's boarding house in Groton.

Bristol Bill's real name was William Darlington. He was born in the English port of Bristol, where he first achieved notoriety as a bank robber. Bristol Bill loved to dress up as a gentleman—in embroidered vests, silk ties, beautifully cut woolen trousers and coat, even a black formal tophat, white gloves, and always carrying a gold-headed walking stick. And, of course, a gun. Bristol Bill would swagger into a bank, tip his hat to any ladies present, rap his stick on the counter to gain attention, and announce, "I'm Bristol Bill and you are being robbed. Kindly cooperate so that I need spill no blood!"

From the beginning, Bristol Bill seemed intent on establishing a reputation as a gentlemanly bandit, one with exquisite manners and an eye for the ladies. He never robbed a lady, and gentlemen unfortunate enough to be in a bank when Bristol Bill showed up were allowed to keep their watches and jewelry as long at they handed over their cash promptly.

Eventually, Bill decided that printing his own cash was less risky than robbing banks. He became a counterfeiter, but his fakes were not particularly artistic or convincing. With the English police hot on his trail, Bristol Bill sailed for America. It was his belief that American paper money, which then was issued by a bewildering variety of local banks, would be easier to counterfeit.

Flamboyant Bristol Bill, however, had a character flaw that, for a counterfeiter, was a serious problem. He did not pay attention to details, like spelling. Allegedly he once printed a batch of fake five dollar notes on which "dollar" was spelled "doller"! When banks and merchants refused to change his money for gold or silver coins, Bristol Bill lost his cool. He began forcing banks at gunpoint to exchange gold for his obvious counterfeits. Gone was the carefully cultivated image of a gentleman bandit. He successfully evaded police in big cities, but was caught, to his outrage, in the backcountry village of Groton. At his trial in the county courthouse in St. Johnsbury, he managed to sneak a knife into court. He attacked and killed the state's attorney right in the courtroom. Bristol Bill was hanged for this offense.

They say that the ghost of Bristol Bill, hanged in 1850, still prowls the little village, the scene of his humiliating capture. You'll recognize his ghost if you see it. It is of a finely dressed Victorian gentleman angrily brandishing a bloody knife. Stay well clear of old Bristol Bill—he's still angry about being caught by a Vermont village constable after evading capture by big city police forces on both sides of the Atlantic.

The Sleeping Ghost

Vermont seems to have more than its fair share of truly unusual ghosts. There is the case of the sleeping ghost, for example. Ghosts have been seen in many poses or engaged in various activities, but a ghost who appears to be sound asleep surely is a rarity. Vermont's "sleeping ghost" is supposed to be the spirit of William Scott, the most famous army private of the Civil War. Oddly, Scott's fame is based on the fact that he fell asleep.

A large granite marker stands beside the William Scott Memorial Highway, that section of U.S. Route 302 between East Barre and Boltonville. This slab of Vermont granite marks Scott's birthplace, and it also is the site of alleged appearances by his ghost.

Private William Scott was only 22-years-old when he was caught sleeping at his sentry post at Camp Lyon on the Potomac. Since this was a clear example of dereliction of duty in wartime, Scott was court-martialed. He was found guilty and sentenced to die before a firing squad. What made Private Scott nationally famous as the "sleeping sentinel" in the words of the newspapers was what happened next. Scott's comrades carried his plight directly to the commander-in-chief, petitioning President Lincoln to spare the young soldier's life. Their petition was so eloquently persuasive that Lincoln personally interviewed Scott. It turned out that Private Scott admitted falling asleep, to his great regret and shame, but there were extenuating circumstances. Scott had been on sentry duty the entire previous night, having taken the place of a sick comrade. Private Scott had not had any rest for nearly thirty-five hours but had not refused an order to stand sentry duty a second night in a row.

President Lincoln was not a stranger to difficult decisions on life and death, but his humanitarian nature led him to overturn the army order and pardon William Scott. At the time, this proved to be a controversial move, as many believed that Lincoln's leniency would undermine army morale, encouraging more inattention to duty or even desertion. The incident became national news, with many strong feeling on both sides.

A year later, William Scott was killed by a Confederate bullet at the Battle of Lee's Mill, Virginia. The fact that he died valiantly in defense of the Union made him a hero. It also vindicated Abraham Lincoln's humanity and judgment. And so the spirit of William Scott sleeps on, a symbol of forgiveness as well as of valor in war. Should you spot his ghost, just tiptoe quietly away.

The Ghost of the Black Dog

An old farmhouse near Barre is said to be haunted by an unusual ghost—that of a black spaniel. How the ghost came about is an interesting case of a family dispute. The question that divided the family is a common one: Do ghosts exist or not?

The story is that the elderly patriarch of the family was a firm believer in things supernatural. He was convinced that ghosts were quite real. He also believed in physical reincarnation, witchcraft, vampires, and UFOs. The rest of his family were equally strongly convinced skeptics.

The nonbelievers in the family did not argue their point with any passion, as they didn't want to upset the old man, who incidentally controlled the family money. As the old man became increasingly frail, and it was evident that death was near, he became ever more firmly convinced that reincarnation was in his destiny. To the consternation of his loved ones, the old man fixated on the belief that his soul would enter the body of his dog, a black cocker spaniel named Max. He begged his family to promise that, after the old man's death, Max would have a permanent and pampered home with them.

Evidently with fingers crossed behind their backs, his family agreed. Soon after the old man had died and made his final journey to the grave, the family took Max to the veterinarian to be put to sleep. That's when the trouble began.

No amount of scrubbing, deodorizing, or burning scented candles could rid the house of the old familiar doggy odor. Long black hairs continued to infest Max's favorite lounging spots on the carpets and upholstered furniture. Ghostly barks still announced the arrival of the mailman. As was Max's habit in life, a cold, wet nose still nuzzled the older son in the morning to awaken him, but of course there was no dog there.

Max had been sent to dog heaven because the family members were eerily concerned that the dog would remind them of the old man's superstitions and weird beliefs. Was Max now a ghost? And was it the spirit of the dog, or the reincarnated phantom of the old man? Was Max haunting them in revenge for his untimely death, or was the old man wreaking revenge for their breaking their pledge to give Max a comfortable life, with or without containing the soul of his master?

One last incident drove the family from the house and led to its sale to another. A family friend made them a present of a puppy. The puppy bounded into the house, full of innocent joy in life and eager to make friends. Suddenly, the pup froze like a statue, then yelped as though being attacked. The puppy ran out the door, ears pinned back, whining, and cowered in a distant field. Nothing would persuade the little dog to reenter the house. Had Max's ghost terrified the pup? The family didn't stay to find an answer.

The Double Who Foretold Death

They used to tell this story up around Swanton. A farmer and expert carpenter, Jim Cross, was out walking alone in the woods in the summer of 1850. Gradually, he became aware that someone, or something, was walking on a parallel course through the dense underbrush. Just a little uneasy at the possibility that he was being followed for some reason, Jim altered course to bring him closer to the other walker in the woods.

Eventually he saw another man approaching, who raised a reassuring hand in greeting. As the two got closer, Jim realized that this man closely resembled himself. On face-to-face inspection, the other man looked precisely like Jim. He was looking at his own double. Jim was too astonished to speak, but his double broke the tense silence.

"You have exactly one year to live," intoned the double. "Have no fear, but prepare yourself for death." And at that, the double abruptly disappeared. Badly shaken, Jim sat down on a stump to consider this revelation. As far as he knew, he was still in good health, a vigorous thirty-eight-years-old. He confided his experience to his wife, who told no one, and his mother who told only a few of her closest friends. Within a week, the whole community had offered sympathy and support.

As his predicted lifespan grew short, Jim noticed that friends and relatives were uneasy about spending time in his company. Jim guessed, probably correctly, that others were nervous about being close to him. What if Jim was to be struck by lightening or flattened by a runaway team of horses? It wouldn't pay to be close to a doomed man, as clearly, Jim's untimely death would be a result of an accident—he remained in robust health.

On the day his mysterious double had predicted to be his last, there was a barn raising on a neighbor's farm. Out of courtesy, Jim and his wife were invited. Jim brought along his carpenter's toolbox, but no one wished to work alongside him. "It's too dangerous," they would say, referring to the work but clearly meaning being close to a doomed man. Jim eventually gave up trying to join a work crew. He wandered off into a field by himself. Spying a bunch of violets, his wife's favorite, growing by a jumble of boulders, Jim stooped to gather them. As he did so, a rattlesnake hidden among the rocks suddenly struck him in the throat. The venom reached his brain in seconds, and Jim fell dead.

His story was told and retold as an example of the fatalistic proverb that when one's time is come, it comes, regardless of one's actions. Pray that you never meet your double face-to-face.

Barre Vampire

Around 1822, the people of Barre became convinced that a vampire dwelt among them. Perhaps he was a Scots stonecutter employed in the new granite quarries then springing up, one Joe MacIntosh. Their suspicion of Joe was based on two facts: He was a "foreigner" and, more importantly, his first wife had died of consumption, and his second wife appeared to be in declining health also.

Consumption was the nineteenth-century term for tuberculosis. TB was much dreaded, known to be communicable, and usually fatal. Doctors were helpless in the face of this disease and avoided such a diagnosis if at all possible, and thus escape close and frequent contact with the doomed victim.

When Joe MacIntosh's first bride, a vigorously healthy farm girl in her late teens, began to lose weight and develop a pale, milky, almost translucent skin, becoming lethargic and melancholy, her doctor suspected tuberculosis but delayed diagnosing her condition as such, knowing that most regarded it as a death sentence. She literally wasted away and eventually was buried. Joe's second wife, like his first, came to the marriage the picture of blooming youth, brimming with vitality and good cheer. Yet, within months, she began taking on the wan image of bloodless lassitude. Could it be, by some horrible coincidence, that the second Mrs. MacIntosh would follow her predecessor to an early grave? Or were both women the victim of something more sinister than consumption? Was their lifeblood being drained by a vampire? Vermonters of the time had a different perception of vampires than the classic East European version personified by Dracula. Local folks thought that a vampire's victims became vampires following their deaths. The first Mrs. MacIntosh's coffin was dug up and opened. Sure enough, her flesh was that of a robustly healthy woman. Most damning was the fact that her mouth was full of fresh blood!

The Vermont prescription for killing a vampire did not involve a wooden stake through the heart. Instead, the corpse was decapitated and the head and heart burned on a blacksmith's forge. Joe's second wife immediately began her recovery. But who was the original vampire who victimized the first wife and made her a vampire in death? The townspeople kept a close eye on Joe, but no other vampire activity was ever seen again in Barre. Still, it might be a good idea to watch your neighbors for sudden weight loss and skin like skimmed milk. You never know.

The House That Bled

Arson is illegal, no exceptions, no excuses, unless, perhaps, the arson is not for gain but to destroy a house made unlivable by the presence of a monstrous evil. Many years ago, the owner of a house in Woodbury believed that he had no choice but to burn his accursed house to the ground, as the house had witnessed a truly horrific crime.

A successful local businessman and investor had decided to sell his interest in a thriving granite quarry on the flanks of Woodbury Mountain. He had just turned fifty, and his young wife recently had given birth to twin boys. It was time, he decided, to simplify his life by selling some of the business interests that had required so much of his attention.

Some business interests down in Barre, where granite quarrying also was carried out on a grand scale, were in the mood to acquire more top-quality reserves such as those of Woodbury Mountain. His trip to Barre was to close the deal. He insisted on being paid in gold coin, as the country was going through yet another of those nineteenth-century financial panics and paper money was suspect.

Unfortunately, an unscrupulous clerk at the bank in Barre who had handed over a bag of gold to the Woodbury man decided to follow him on the train and wait for an opportunity to take the small fortune for himself. The would-be thief followed his victim home from the train station and waited until the early morning hours when he thought the household would be sound asleep. Breaking into the house as quietly as possible, the burglar found the gold and was about to sneak away when the young mother was awakened by her hungry infants. It was time for a feeding. The burglar was discovered. In a panic, he beat the woman to death with a heavy candlestick. Then, his ears filled with the screams of two babies with empty stomachs, he seized each infant in turn by the legs and, swinging them like a baseball bat, smashed their skulls against the wall. Their father, finally awakened by their screams, attempted to attack the invader, but was himself knocked down and out by a blow to the head.

When the horrible scene was discovered by the arrival of the couple's housemaid, the walls were literally dripping blood. The man recovered from his ordeal in the physical sense, but not in his mental health. He could never forget the sight of his murdered family and the walls covered in gore. His nightmares never ended as, according to legend, the house began to bleed. Every morning fresh blood would be found, oozing down the walls. Every day, the house would be scrubbed clean, but every night the blood would return.

Finally, the man set fire to his house, destroying forever the bleeding walls that had witnessed such a brutal night. Wouldn't you burn it down yourself?

Stalked by a UFO

A UFO once stalked a woman on her commute from her secretarial job in Barre to her home in the remote little community of East Orange. Although badly shaken by the experience, she didn't report it to the police, nor did she talk about it until, years later, she heard a similar story from a trusted friend. How many such encounters never are reported officially or, indeed, never mentioned at all?

UFOlogists, as they call themselves, believe that spotting unidentified flying objects actually is a much more common experience than many would believe. If, as many suppose, UFOs are in fact visitors from other worlds rather than secret experimental craft created on this planet, is there a real possibility that we are the objects of curiosity or scientific examination by life-forms from other planets?

Before UFO reports are dismissed as some sort of hoax, these facts should be considered. Reports of phenomena outside of the official wisdom of science should not be automatically dismissed. A few centuries ago, for example, scientists scoffed at the idea that rocks of extraterrestrial origin could fall from the sky. But they do. They're called meteorites. People who report sighting UFOs often are derided as unreliable or worse, yet President Jimmy Carter claims he saw one. Two Vermonters hiking together in the woods reported a UFO encounter a few years ago. One was the Roman Catholic bishop of Vermont, the other was a former governor of Vermont. But even expressing interest in the possibility for UFOs can bring scorn and bad jokes.

At any rate the East Orange commuter shouldn't have hesitated to tell her tale. In midwinter, it was already dark when she left the office in downtown Barre. Traffic thinned considerably after she turned off U.S. Route 302 to follow Highway 25 down the valley of the Waits River. Suddenly, a disklike flying object of gleaming silver, outlined in rapidly blinking white lights, was hovering above her pickup. When she accelerated, it accelerated. When she slowed to a crawl, it did likewise. She pulled over and stopped. The UFO hovered above, and then, terrifyingly, it slowly descended toward her. In a panic, she burned rubber, doing a jackrabbit takeoff down the road. The UFO followed. Then to the woman's astonished relief, the mysterious craft suddenly veered off to the east, apparently to join or follow a second UFO now visible in the night sky. She often wonders just what would have happened if the UFO that was stalking her hadn't zoomed off in the wake of the second one.

The Ghost Skier of Stowe

Many skiers would like to believe that, if they've been very, very good, the destination of their souls after death will be Vermont—in winter, of course, and, for choice, ski slopes like those of Stowe, close by Vermont's highest peak, Mount Mansfield, at 4,393 feet.

However many spirits would like to hang out at Stowe, at least one has succeeded in doing exactly that, if the legend is to be believed. One popular theory about ghosts is that they haunt the place where the living person was happiest, the perfect match of geography and personality. Stowe's resident ghost is said to be that of a longtime ski instructor and self-appointed protector of the slopes, an Austrian immigrant who first came to Stowe in the 1930s and died in the 1960s.

Max (his last name has been lost over the years) was a refugee from the Nazi takeover of Austria in 1936. Austrians are right up there with Norwegians and Swiss in their enthusiasm for, and skills in, skiing. For Max, Vermont must have seemed close to paradise, with places like Stowe already famous as a ski resort and plentiful job opportunities for experienced skiers. Vermont's mountain slopes and snows were matched, as far as Max was concerned, by its political culture. Outraged by Nazi atrocities, Vermont's legislature declared war on Germany two months before the U.S. did so. And so, for Max, the quaintly picturesque village of Stowe with its multiple ski slopes (currently forty-seven in number) combined with its hostility to the hated Nazis was the perfect setting for the man and, eventually, his spirit.

It is soon after dawn on one of those crystalline clear blue sky days that follow a snowstorm. The red-clad skier seems to rocket down Stowe's most challenging, expert level slope. He is checking for any hazards like wind-blown, downed trees or potential avalanche conditions. His grace and speed impress any early risers who see him flash down the mountain. And then they notice that

his passage leaves no trail in the fresh snow. Did they really see him? They look again and see only fresh, unmarked powder. The ghost skier is out again, savoring the tremendous freedom of skiing and at the same time trying to ensure a good safe thrill for the thousands to follow in his (nonexistent) tracks. Good show, Max.

The Strangest Ghost of All

In Calais, a tiny community north of Montpelier, folks used to spot the ghost of Pardon Janes, a man who, in life, probably was the Green Mountain State's champion eccentric. Vermont has been home to a long list of highly individualistic people, so that when Vermonters regard a person to be eccentric, they are eccentric indeed! Now Pardon Janes's phantom hasn't been seen very often as of late, but if really odd apparitions are your thing, perhaps you'll be lucky at Calais.

You'll know Pardon's ghost when you see him. He'll be dressed in clean but humble clothing in the style of the mid-nineteenth century (Pardon Janes was born in 1788 and died in 1870). This spirit will ignore you completely, not unusual for ghosts but also typical of the living man. What made the man, and his ghost, distinctive is a short pitchfork strapped to his right hand. Janes used his pitchfork as a means of avoiding any contact with another person. The sharpened tines of his pitchfork served twin purposes. No one wished to get too close to the razor-sharp fork, and thus dealt with Janes literally at arm's length, which is the way Pardon Janes wanted it. Also, the pitchfork was a kind of primitive artificial hand, enabling the eccentric to transact business without touching anyone, or anything, directly.

For example, when Pardon went to the local general store, a note listing his requirements would be carefully detached from the points of the pitchfork by the clerk, who'd then fill the order. The clerk would take money from a pail hanging from the fork, and place Janes's order and his change in the pail. Not one word was exchanged during these transactions.

Interestingly, Pardon Janes was not at all strange in his younger days. As a young man, he was known for his sociability, his intelligence, and his lively and persuasive speaking talents. His neighbors respected him enough to elect him to the state legislature. But, it seems, almost overnight, Pardon withdrew from human contact, literally. He became a hermit, living by himself on his farm, and venturing to the store only when necessary and doing that in silence as described.

No one was certain what had brought about this change in Pardon. There was, however, a rumor that he had lusted after many lovely young women in the neighborhood, so much so that the devil himself had warned Pardon to keep his hands to himself or be dragged down into hell. Had Pardon Janes taken this warning a bit too literally? We'll never know. Remember to stay clear of that pitchfork if you should encounter the ghost of Pardon Janes. Those points are sharp.

Connecticut River Valley

THIS LONG, NARROW REGION FOLLOWS THE CONNECTICUT RIVER northward from the Massachusetts border to McIndoe Falls and includes the cities of Brattleboro, Windsor, and White River Junction. Vermont's first constitution was written at Windsor. Because early explorers followed waterways, the Connecticut River Valley was the scene of the first English settlement in Vermont, Fort Dummer. The valley always has been an important transportation route; in fact, Interstate 91 now runs along it.

The Shade of the Sage of Woodstock

A ghost, or "shade" as they were called in olden times, has been known to stroll the streets of Woodstock, one of Vermont's most picturesque villages. Many believe that this apparition actually is the shade of the Sage of Woodstock—George Perkins Marsh. George was born in Woodstock on March 15, 1801, and died July 23, 1882, after a long and distinguished career as a congressman, diplomat, and author of twenty books. It was his book *Man and Nature: The Earth as Modified by Human Action* that still is considered the fountainhead of the conservation movement in the United States. Perhaps it is a fitting monument to this native son pioneer in promoting the protection of the natural environment that Vermont became one of the first states to enact "growth management" statewide. This law protects natural resources and sets new goals in land preservation and controlled, planned growth of housing and urban areas. Even earlier, in 1970, Vermont's legislature passed an environmental control law enabling the state to limit major developments that could detract from Vermont's justly famed rural scenic charm. George Marsh would have been so proud.

Marsh graduated from Dartmouth College at the age of nineteen. A young man in a hurry, he was a three-term congressman before being appointed U.S. Minister to Turkey, after which he taught at Columbia University, where he earned a reputation as a leading intellectual. President Lincoln appointed him the first U.S. Minister to the Kingdom of Italy, newly united under the leadership of the great King Victor Emmanuel. Marsh kept the post for twenty-one years, becoming a close friend and advisor to the King.

It is said that Marsh's ghost generally is a benign one, content to stroll about Woodstock's town square, politely tipping his hat to the ladies. Should anyone approach too closely, the ghost simply disappears. But a decidedly hostile, frowning spirit has been known to harass those favoring uncontrolled development. The author of *Man and Nature* believed in the harmonious interaction of the two, and woe to those who would ignore Marsh's principles of intelligent and sensitive planning.

In his lifetime, George Marsh had earned such a fine reputation as a conservationist and geographer that he frequently was called as an expert witness before Congressional committees. Only once was his sage advice ignored, fortunately for everyone as it turned out. A committee considering Russia's offer to sell us Alaska invited Marsh to offer his expert opinion as a geographer and conservationist. Not a good idea, advised George Marsh, mentioning it would be the first time the U.S. acquired non-contiguous (not physically adjacent) territory. Besides, said Marsh, Alaska's only known resource was its fur-bearing animals, which had been so ruthlessly hunted by the Russians as to be in danger of extermination. As a result, advised Marsh, Alaska was, in his words, a "sucked orange"—a vast empty land drained of its value.

Luckily for Alaska, and the rest of the U.S., Marsh was for once ignored. Should you by chance encounter the shade of the Sage of

Woodstock, don't mention Alaska. He's still sensitive about his one great misjudgment. And don't let him catch you with a chainsaw in your hands—he is still our first conservationist at heart.

Captain Morey's Phantom Steamboat

The shrill whistle of a steamboat echoes eerily across the little moonlit, fog-shrouded lake. Those who have seen the rather primitive-looking steamer, and there have been many over the years, report that the boat slips quietly through the fog. Her churning paddlewheel creates no wake. Only the mournful steam whistle breaks the silence as the boat turns this way and that on an endless and seemingly erratic voyage in a small, secluded lake surrounded by mountains. It is as though the hands on the wheel are restless and uncertain and the ship's course is unknown. Are the abrupt and repeated turns and backtracking evidence of the captain's frustrations? The steamboat can't find its way out of the lake, and its captain can't find the fame and recognition that should be his.

The scene is Lake Morey near the little town of Fairlee in the Connecticut Valley. The steamboat's captain, builder, and inventor is Samuel Morey, who, as real Vermonters know, was the true inventor of the first practical steamboat.

No, Robert Fulton's *Clermont,* launched in 1807 on the Hudson River, was not the first steamboat. It was the first commercially successful steamboat, and Fulton and his financial backer, Robert Livingston, were very good at publicizing the *Clermont,* but they had company among several other inventors who claimed their own "firsts." Engineer John Fitch launched a forty-five-foot long steamboat on the Delaware River near Philadelphia in 1787, a full twenty years before *Clermont's* maiden voyage from New York City to Albany. Fitch's steamboat was propelled awkwardly by rows of oars rather than a paddlewheel. It worked, but not very well. Pioneer inventor John Stevens of Hoboken, New Jersey, built his first steamboat in 1798. Vermont's native son Captain Samuel Morey operated a tiny steamboat (it could hold only its captain-creator) on the Connecticut River as early as 1793.

Why have few outside Vermont ever heard of Samuel Morey and his steamboat, and why does the ghost of this inventor still pilot

his last steamboat across Lake Morey once a month on the evening of the full moon? Many ghost stories feature a restless, tormented, and frustrated soul who just cannot rest in peace. Life wronged the Captain, or so he believes. In life, Captain Morey was an extremely frustrated man, a classic example of a man far ahead of his time in his scientific genius. It also is evident that he was a far better inventor than he was a businessman, and perhaps he was much too trusting of other men, like Robert Fulton, for example.

The local legend is that Samuel Morey traveled to New York City once to show his models of a steamboat to Robert Fulton and Robert Livingston. Fulton already had built one steamboat in an attempt to obtain a French patent on the idea. This 1803 version was launched on the Seine River in Paris, where it promptly sank, a result of Fulton's underestimate of the weight of the engine. Many Vermont supporters of Sam Morey believe that Fulton appropriated Morey's ideas and designs for his own *Clermont* in 1802. It is clear that Morey's concept of a large, powerful, and reliable steamboat was adapted in the 1808 debut of the steamboat *Vermont* on Lake Champlain. *Vermont* was 120 feet long, 20 feet wide, 167 tons, and was the second commercially successful steamboat ever built in the U.S.

In the meantime, Captain Morey continued to experiment with steamboats. A bitterly disappointed and frustrated man, he deliberately sank his last prototype steamboat in Lake Morey, abandoning his efforts.

Morey later devoted his imagination and engineering talents to designing a gasoline-powered internal combustion engine, for which he received a patent in 1826—more than half a century ahead of the earliest experiments of others. Perhaps it is possible to be so far ahead of one's time that one is written off as a dreamer rather than credited with inventive genius.

At any rate, Captain Morey's last steamboat, or at least its ghost, rises monthly from the bottom of Lake Morey to once again sail under the command of the great captain himself. Should you hear its ghostly whistle some moonlit night, salute the steamboat and wish the spirit of the embittered captain well. And don't mention the name of Robert Fulton around Lake Morey.

Springfield's Haunted Bridge

Springfield was built in the narrow valley of the Black River, a short distance from the place where the Black joins the Connecticut River. There at Springfield, the Black River flows through a narrow gorge before plunging over a waterfall. The river always had been the reason that people were attracted to the area. The Abnaki Indians discovered that the swirling pool of deep water below the falls was a great place to fish. But woe to any fisherman who fell in the water, for they would never be seen again. When the first Europeans on the scene inquired as to the name of the river, the local Abnaki replied that it was the Black, or Dark River, because of its dark reputation. The Black River provided fish in abundance, but also claimed the souls of unwary fishermen.

The white settlers of Springfield were attracted more by the falls than the fish, for they saw the potential water power of a swift river churning through a steep and narrow gorge. Springfield became an important manufacturing center. Now the same tumbling white waters, with their swift currents that powered the mill wheels, also had a dark side. They split the little town in two, as the only safe way to ferry across the racing waters was to go downstream to French Meadows near the mouth of the Black River. Don't tempt the evil spirits of the gorge, advised the Abnaki.

The necessity of a bridge was clear. William Lockwood, who built the first mill on the river there, also built the first bridge. To demonstrate that a bridge was possible, he simply felled a towering hemlock tree across the gorge, intending to later build a proper bridge. It is a local legend that a blind man tapping along with his cane crossed the river on that one tree trunk, completely unaware of the danger he was in. After that experience, which happened back in 1774, a proper bridge was built.

Due to a combination of neglect and wood rot, an early, wooden version of this bridge began to fall apart. Timbers parted and fell into the river below one stormy, moonless night. The town doctor, called on an emergency to the opposite side of town, approached the teetering remnants of the bridge, unaware that it was close to total collapse. Neither the doctor nor his horse could see in the pitch blackness. However, they could hear the steady tap-tapping sound of a cane striking the timbers as someone—or something—

crossed safely ahead of him. The horse confidently followed the tapping sound and the doctor's carriage crossed the river—on swaying timbers only six inches wider than the carriage's wheel span!

To this day, many Springfield residents believe that the blind man's ghost has become the guardian spirit of the bridge, ensuring everyone of a safe passage even under dangerous conditions.

Two Contrasting Indian Ghosts

In the tiny village of South Newbury, in the Oxbow Cemetery, lie the remains of two Abnaki Indians. Their ghosts, both of whom appear to haunt the cemetery are as different as could be. The ghost of Old Joe is a helpful spirit, for it is said that he appears only to point lost travelers in the right direction, then quickly dissolves into a mist.

The other Native American ghost, that of Captain John, is a fierce warrior, brandishing a tomahawk with righteous fury. In his life, Captain John had been a warrior, a judge, and an executioner.

In the vicinity of Newbury, the Connecticut River makes great double bends within a wide valley, creating broad, lush riverside meadows known as the Oxbow Meadows. There the Abnaki Indians farmed and fished for a living, supporting a large population. Old Joe was a peaceful Indian, who welcomed the white settlers coming up the Connecticut Valley and served as a guide to many of them. His friendship and services as a guide led to the state's granting him a pension of $70 a year, a nice sum in the late 18th century, and perhaps the reason for his conscientious continuing service as a guide.

Captain John led an interesting and varied life. During the French and Indian Wars, John fought on the French side against British General Braddock. He claimed to have come close to shooting one of Braddock's colonial lieutenants, George Washington. During the Revolution, Captain John fought with the Americans against British General Burgoyne. The grateful Americans appointed him a judge, specifically to judge disputes within the St. Francis band of Abnaki.

A local Indian called Toomalek attempted to kill the warrior who had run off with Toomalek's betrothed future wife, but because of his poor aim, Toomalek accidentally killed the girl instead. Captain

John, acting as judge, ruled that it was an accidental homicide, as Toomalek clearly meant no harm to her. Toomalek later was accused of tomahawking the man his bullet had missed. Captain John ruled that there was no evidence nor eyewitness to this crime and again acquitted Toomalek. Toomalek, apparently convinced he could get away with anything, next killed Captain John's son. There was a witness this time. Captain John judged Toomalek guilty, appointed himself executioner, and shot Toomalek on the spot. Don't mess with the judge, and don't fool around with his ghost either.

The Ghost of the Westminster Massacre

The tiny village of Westminster, ironically named for England's seat of government, was host to the convention that, on January 15, 1777, declared Vermont to be a free and independent state in rebellion against King George the Third of England. Westminster can also claim to be the site of the first military engagement of the Revolution, the so-called Westminster Massacre, which took place on March 13, 1775.

As a massacre, it doesn't rate very highly, as the list of dead patriots adds up to three. One, William French, died instantly, and two others received wounds that led to their deaths within days. The Westminster Massacre was, however, far more significant than its death toll might suggest, as it aroused the righteous fury of Vermonters against King George's government. And that massacre produced the very first patriotic ghost of the Revolution.

The Westminster Massacre happened because a group of patriots seized control of the courthouse and refused admission to His Majesty's appointed officials. Those officials went and got the local sheriff and some soldiers. That night, with no warning, the soldiers fired their guns into the courthouse, killing William French, and wounding several others. William is buried in the old cemetery at the north end of the village. His headstone, an exact replica of the original that was destroyed when the church burned down, has a long description of how he was shot "by the hands of cruel ministerial tools of George ye Third." Across the road from William

French's grave is a rather curious monument to his memory. It is a great chair carved out of white marble. It is said that William French's ghost much prefers to sit in this chair to lying in his grave. His ghost often appears in his chair at dawn and dusk. This completely relaxed spirit seems to enjoy sitting and watching the world go by and never bothers anyone. The ghost does stand up, however, and come to attention whenever an American flag happens to pass by. William French, the first martyr to the cause of American freedom, is a very patriotic ghost.

Still Counting Her Money

Employees at the bank in Bellows Falls didn't talk about it, at least openly. Bankers are supposed to maintain an image of unflappable sobriety; they are not supposed to see ghosts, especially ghosts in their bank. Although this spirit hasn't been seen recently, she is alleged to have haunted the bank vault for years after her death.

More than one banker was astonished to find, as the vault was opened at the start of a business day, the figure of an elderly woman seated on the floor of the vault. She is surrounded by stacks of currency, piles of stocks and bonds, portfolios of mortgages, and trays of gold coins. She is counting, over and over again, her vast wealth. But as daylight penetrates the opened vault, the woman and her worldly goods evaporate as the morning mist.

The observers had no doubt whatever as to whose shade they saw, as in life, the old woman liked to do exactly what her ghost was doing—gloating over the proof of her wealth. She was Henrietta Robinson Green, better known as Hetty Green, a.k.a., the Witch of Wall Street. In her day (she was born in 1834 and died in 1916) she was the richest woman in America. Not only was she super rich, but she had a genius for making money that was envied by the Wall Street bankers and brokers whom she routinely outsmarted.

Hetty was born rich, the daughter of a Bellows Falls merchant who'd made one fortune in whaling and another in the China trade. Hetty admired her successful father and was an eager student of his financial prowess. She hugely increased the fortune she inherited by energetic trading in stocks, bonds, and real estate. People called her the Witch of Wall Street because she seemed to possess an uncanny ability to predict the future. Hetty always foresaw bank panics, stock market crashes, and the collapse of real estate "bubbles," cashing out just before the collapse. Some even wondered if she actually possessed satanic powers in foretelling the future.

The richer she grew, the more Hetty hated to spend money. She was notorious for wanting to bargain with local merchants, seldom willingly paying the asking price. Sadly, when her only son had an infected sore on his leg, Hetty dragged him from doctor to doctor, trying to bargain down the cost of treatment. The delay in medical care resulted in an amputation. Perhaps predictably, that son grew up to be a big spender, living a lavish lifestyle that would have horrified Hetty.

Maybe Hetty was bewitched by money, a victim of the compulsion to pile up more and more wealth so that she could count her stocks, bonds, money, and mortgages as she sat in the bank vault. In death as in life, Hetty seemed mesmerized by the climbing numbers in her account books. Her ghost must have visited her money in the bank vault because Hetty had finally realized that she couldn't take it with her into the spirit world.

Be careful if you are assigned to open the bank vault in Bellows Falls.

Gasping for Breath at Brattleboro

These ghosts, and there seem to be several of them, are heard, but not seen. It can be a very frightening experience to hear the agonizing, labored sounds of someone, or something, struggling for breath. Everyone has had at least a brief moment when they couldn't breath normally. Nothing else causes so much instant panic, so everyone can identify with the poor souls momentarily deprived of fresh air.

These ghostly sounds of frantic, hoarse attempts to gulp in air are said to have originated in the rather sadistic practices once inflicted on mental patients at the old Brattleboro Retreat, a state-supported hospital for the insane. Founded here in 1836, the retreat was typical of nineteenth-century mental institutions in that experimental treatments were imposed on helpless patients in the absence of any truly scientific understanding of their illnesses.

Brattleboro's retreat facility was established in an era of water cures, or hydrotherapy. The basic idea was that "taking the waters" was a long-established, even ancient general cure for a variety of ailments. Since Roman times, Europeans had visited mineral springs to drink, and bathe in, the supposedly curative waters. Brattleboro boasted its own hydropathic establishment, a blend of luxury hotel resort and clinic, between 1845 and 1870. Wealthy guests came to "cure" a variety of ailments ranging from gout and arthritis to digestive complaints and impotence. Many left convinced that the mineral waters had helped them. Whether the "cures" worked or not, it was a nice excuse for a country vacation being pampered by an attentive staff.

Unfortunately for many mentally ill patients, the popularity of the mineral waters suggested that the water cure might restore mental health. The approach, however, was a brutal treatment compared to the luxury spa enjoyed by rich hypochondriacs at the hydropathic establishment nearby. At the state-run retreat, patients were bound in restraints and repeatedly dunked into large tubs of cold water. Brief, but terrifying total immersions left them sputtering and gasping for breath.

It is said that the victim's screams could be heard for great distances, and that many employees at the retreat quit after witnessing the hydrotherapy sessions. The ghostly pathetic struggles for air still can be heard on still nights, according to some. These phantom gasps are among the most truly frightening encounters with the supernatural imaginable.

The Dummer Ghosts

The "Dummer Ghosts" refer to their location, not their level of intelligence. Although the name sounds like a bad joke, Fort Dummer, established in 1724, was the first permanent European settlement in Vermont. This fort was named for Massachusetts's lieutenant governor, Sir William Dummer. Sir Dummer (whose name must have given him an absolutely miserable childhood) wanted to reinforce Massachusetts's claim to what is now Vermont, which also was claimed by the colonies of New York and New Hampshire. This confusion over exactly which colony owned Vermont was the fault of careless wording of land grants by the British government.

Fort Dummer most likely really was a dumb idea if it was intended to protect Massachusetts's claims to territory against New

Hampshire and New York's claims. Eventually, King George the Third decreed that New Hampshire's western boundary was the Connecticut River, allowing New York to claim Vermont (but Vermonters disagreed strongly). Fort Dummer was built out of pine logs and was 180 feet square. As far as anyone knows, the fort never was attacked by anyone and was dismantled in 1763. The town of Brattleboro was established about a mile from the site of the fort in 1753.

And so Fort Dummer never needed to be built, was never involved in a battle, and soon was abandoned. Life at Fort Dummer must have been boring, to say the least.

Appropriately for a fort that never was necessary, the site of Fort Dummer now is under water, drowned when the Vernon Dam was built on the Connecticut River. Strangely, Fort Dummer's ghosts didn't appear until the site was underwater. One theory is that some early graves at the fort were covered by the rising waters, antagonizing the spirits of the deceased. Now, or so some locals claim, the faintly phosphorescent, glowing forms of the dead can be seen moving slowly underwater around the submerged foundations of the old fort. Whenever these aquatic ghosts appear, it is said, there is no use fishing for the fish all stay clear of the ghosts. Fort Dummer really was a bummer.

The Bellows Falls Daredevil

Old-timers say that Sara Rising Moon still rides her canoe over Bellows Falls once a year, or rather, her spirit does. Bellows Falls, named for early settler Col. Benjamin Bellows and once called the Great Falls of the Connecticut, is where the Connecticut River drops over fifty feet at the town. Although at least a dozen daredevils have survived a trip over and down Bellows Falls, the most famous survivor was Sara, an Abnaki Indian, who apparently went over the falls by accident, but so enjoyed the experience that she deliberately took the plunge several more times in life, and her spirit is said to continue the tradition.

Sara's ghost has to wait for enough water to make her repeat thrill ride, as the falls often are but a mere trickle thanks to the demands of power generation. The falls area had a large Abnaki population before the Europeans arrived on the scene. The pool below the falls would teem with shad and salmon during the migrations of those fish. Indian rock paintings, now almost completely destroyed, and an abundance of arrowheads, pottery shards, and ancient fire-pots testify to a long, dense occupation by the Abnaki people.

Sara should have been very familiar with the hazard of the falls, but one night in 1781, the story goes, she carelessly let her canoe get caught up in the current rushing toward the falls. Sara was rumored to take a little nip of spiritous liquors now and then. On the occasion of her unplanned trip over the falls, she had an open bottle of rum with her. When she realized, at last, her plight as the canoe was carried toward the brink, she decided that it was too late to avert tragedy and she might as well finish the bottle. Sara chugged down the rest of the rum and lay down in the canoe to await her fate.

"Yahoo!" she yelled as her canoe went over the edge in the foaming torrent. "Yippee!" Minutes later a very drunk, very happy, and very, very lucky Sara was pulled from the water at the base of the falls. "That was such fun!" she exclaimed.

And to this very day, on warm summer evenings as the water level permits, one can hear "Yahoo! Yippee!" echoing over the falls as Sara goes for another thrill ride. She really would have enjoyed amusement park roller coasters.

The Spirits of the Love Communists

Ghosts tend to be solitary, entirely alone in whatever twilight existence they inhabit. The merry ghosts of Putney, however, are an exception. These carefree spirits usually appear around dusk in the charming little town, and in small groups from two to four or five. They never attempt to interact with the living, nor are they threatening or scary in any way. Indeed, they seem to be romantically absorbed in one another. If approached by the living, they simply disappear like fog evaporating. They are said to be the phantoms of the perfectionists, an interesting, and at the time, highly controversial cult that made Putney its home about 180 years ago.

This unusual religious group had an influential, charismatic leader in John Humprey Noyes. Noyes was well connected: He was the son of a Vermont congressman and a cousin to President Rutherford Hayes. Born in Brattleboro in 1811, he graduated from Dartmouth College at the age of nineteen and went on to study theology at Yale. He became fascinated by the doctrines of the perfectionists, who advocated living in religious communities that practiced a kind of "Bible Communism"—communal property, communal households, and communal love.

That last communal effort was what really attracted followers. It also attracted controversy and outrage from his neighbors. Noyes called his concept "complex marriage," but it seemed quite simple to his passionate little flock. The only rule governing sex between, or among, perfectionists was that there were no rules. As Noyes often was quoted, "In a holy community there is no more reason why sexual intercourse should be restrained by law, than why eating and drinking should be—and there is as little occasion for shame in one case as in the other."

Noyes and his happy little group of "love communists," as he called them, lived in Putney for nearly a decade—three and four families to a house—before being forced to move to Oneida, New York. Apparently, the perfectionists were good and law abiding neighbors in general, except for that little lapse on marriage vows.

After that carefree decade in Putney, 1837 to 1847, the perfectionists gave up their complex marriage practices "in deference to public sentiment" (and to stay out of jail). This novel communist experiment lived on for awhile, but somehow the appeal had faded. Now we know why the ghosts of the perfectionists always seem to have those secretive little smiles on their faces. They once were living a libertine's dream.

Be Polite to Ghosts

About a century ago, a married couple, we'll call them Richard and Beverly Currier, owned a prosperous apple orchard in the Connecticut Valley near White River Junction. To their regret, they were childless, but thanks to fertile siblings, they had a large number of nieces and nephews. These nieces and nephews did their best to remain on good terms with Uncle Rick and Aunt Bev, as they fancied themselves the heirs to a considerable fortune. Rick and Bev were hard-working farmers and smart investors who bought farms and houses with their profits from apples, turkeys, and maple syrup, all products of their lands. The profits invested were considerable, as the Curriers were what country folk called "tight"—tight with money, that is, very slow to spend any.

As Rick and Bev approached old age, their nieces and nephews entered a kind of contest to see which could become the favorite, and thus most likely heir. Their aunt and uncle basked in the attention, playing off one against another, fully aware that their popularity rested on their wealth.

Richard passed away first. His widow hardly had time to deal with the legal formalities of his death when she too died. All of the Currier's real estate had been willed to the couple's brothers and sisters. All cash monies were to be divided among nieces and nephews. But, as those very eager relatives soon discovered, the Curriers mistrusted banks and had no accounts on deposit. A thorough search of the house provided only a handful of coins and currency. Was a fortune in gold coins buried somewhere on the farm? The nieces and nephews recalled a favorite joke of Rick and Bev's: "Money doesn't grow on trees—except in Vermont!" Was that just a reference to apples and maple sugar, or a hint to look for buried treasure in the orchards?

No treasure map was found, nor any treasure despite many futile hours of digging random holes. Years later, the ghost of an old lady, withered and bent with age, began to be encountered on the old Currier farm, long since sold off to strangers. The phantom would approach passersby at night, holding out her hands as though entreating them to stop and talk with her. Or, as many feared, to beg money. Everyone avoided the old lady, hurrying away if they saw her. Finally, one old neighbor, having quite a few drinks at a local inn, was feeling mellow enough to stop on the road, tip his hat to the lady, and wish her a good evening. The apparition smiled broadly at the courtesy and beckoned the man to follow her into the orchard. She pointed at the base of a large stump and suggested that he dig a hole. He did, and thus found a dozen quart jars filled with $20 gold pieces. It pays to be polite.

The Brattleboro Brewmaster's Ghost

This old industrial town, crowded into a narrow valley and climbing nearby slopes, is home to one of Vermont's happiest ghosts. He is happy because he is a spirit who enjoys a beer, or rather, several beers, and he is a beer expert—a brewmaster in life.

Before the Prohibition era of the 1920s and early 1930s, and before modern refrigeration, every town in America had a brewery, often several breweries. At the time, beer did not keep well nor travel well. It was best consumed fresh. German-born and German-trained brewmaster Franz "Frank" Roesch had settled in Brattleboro and opened a small brewery around the turn of the twentieth century. His handcrafted lager found an appreciative local market and his own horses pulled the wagon loaded with kegs of Frank's best to a half dozen pubs.

The beer was good, business was good, life was good. Then came Prohibition. Frank tried to shift over to making and bottling soft drinks, but his heart wasn't in it. He missed brewing beer. He missed drinking it in the company of friends.

For the first time in his life, Frank deliberately broke the law. His house, a solidly built old Victorian, had a large stone-walled cellar. Frank converted it into what nowadays would be called a brew pub—a small-scale brewery right behind the bar. He even had a secret extension dug in which to house the brewing vats. Soon family and friends who were in on the secret were dropping in for a foaming pint or two of Frank's best. Even the neighborhood cops would have a fresh brew with him. As Frank's German last name was pronounced "rush," that became a kind of password into the beer cellar. "I'm in a rush," or "Can we rush this?" were the phrases that earned a thirsty stranger a cold stein.

Shortly before Prohibition was ended, Frank was called to brewmaster heaven, and his widow had the secret cellar room walled up with the brewing apparatus inside. The house was sold. No sooner had the new owners moved in than they began to hear hammering sounds in the cellar late at night. No one was there when they investigated, but they noticed chisel marks on the new stonework which walled off, unknown to them, the secret brewing room. What was going on?

Neighbors supplied the story of Frank's brew pub. "Maybe Frank's ghost is trying to get back into the brew chamber," they reasoned. Desperate to eliminate the nightly hammering, the owners had the wall torn out. The ghostly hammering stopped.

Had there really been a frustrated ghost trying to reopen the brew cellar? Don't rush to judgment on that.

The Mysterious Playmate

This experience of a three-year-old child with a mysterious playmate, unseen by adults in the household, was relayed on the grounds of anonymity, by that child, now a 25-year-old man.

The family had just moved into a rented house in White River Junction, having just arrived in Vermont. They knew nothing of the house's history, but the house met their needs and the price was right. Mom and Dad were pleased that their three-year-old, Marshall, seemed to adjust happily to his new surroundings. A minor problem was that, in this long established neighborhood, there were few kids of Marshall's age as potential playmates. Marshall was duly enrolled in a preschool "play and learn" group and had plenty of social interaction five mornings a week. Marshall was a bright, imaginative, and outgoing child. He not only did well at preschool, but entertained himself by the hour in solitary play at home. At least his parents thought that it was solitary play, until they learned better.

Marshall was a highly vocal child, always having something to say around kids or adults. His parents observed, though, that he seemed to be carrying on conversations while playing by himself in the toy-strewn enclosed side porch of their new home. He seemed to be responding to a playmate, but no one else was there or was someone, or something, there?

One day, while watching Marshall playing by himself in his favorite, sun-filled toy room, his mother had an odd experience. While Marshall pushed a toy truck about the floor, another large toy seemed to be following along, but with no visible means of propulsion. Then there was the game of rolling a ball across the floor. Marshall was seated, legs outstretched, on the floor. He would roll the ball across the floor. The ball would stop, then reverse course back to Marshall. It was not bouncing off anything. What was going on?

Marshall began to talk about playing with Robby. Robby did this, Robby did that, Robby liked to roll the ball. But Marshall's limited circle of friends and classmates at preschool did not include anyone named Robby.

Then one day the mother asked a neighbor about the history of the house. The previous tenants had left, it seemed to escape the sad memories of that house. Their Down Syndrome son, Robby, had died in that house. As is unfortunately common with victims of Down, Robby had died of respiratory disease. He was in his late teens, but with the mental age of three or four. Robby had been a friendly boy who loved to play by sitting on the floor and rolling a ball back and forth with whoever would play with him.

While Marshall evidently accepted the idea of an unseen playmate without any fear, his parents were uneasy about the presence of a spirit. They consulted a "ghost hunter." This person sat for hours alone in the toy room, meditating, and sometimes talking in a low voice with the never-yet-seen Robby. Robby, the ghost hunter reported, was a benign but confused presence. He couldn't figure out what had happened to his family. The ghost hunter finally assured Robby that his parents had moved across town and gave the ghost easy-to-follow directions.

Robby left. Marshall missed his playmate at first, but then, in the matter-of-fact way of three-year-olds, accepted that Robby really missed his family and had joined them. As an adult, Marshall can still remember his large, sweet-natured playmate who always "hid" by fading away when adults approached. Is it possible that innocent children can accept unquestioningly the presence of a spirit who only wanted to play?

The Witch of Windsor

The little town of Windsor lies on a terrace, an elevated flat that once was the floodplain of the Connecticut River. Windsor's claim to fame rests on its importance in Vermont. Students of witchcraft history know that Windsor has earned a prominent place in the annals of the supernatural as well.

The free and independent state of Vermont was formally created in a constitutional convention held at Windsor from July 2 through

July 8, 1777. At the time, Windsor was the largest town in the new state and remained so at least until after 1820.

So much for Windsor's official claim to fame in the history books. In the annals of witchcraft, Windsor also is famous as the home of Elizabeth Leeds, the Witch of Windsor. Witches put curses on people, especially people who offend the witch in some way. It's what witches do. Elizabeth's reputation as a kind of super witch, however, rests upon her singular achievement of cursing an entire state—indeed, all of New England. Elizabeth Leeds is credited, if that's the word, with causing the worst year, climatically, in Vermont history. Did she really succeed in causing a disastrous year for the whole region, or was it merely a coincidence that the year that Elizabeth cursed, 1816, simply was the result of natural forces beyond the control of any human, or indeed of any witch?

The climate facts are indisputable. The year 1816 came to be known throughout Vermont and its neighbors as the year of the famine. Vermonters joked bitterly that it should have been called "eighteen hundred and froze to death." The typical growing season in the Connecticut Valley, that is, the period between spring's last killing frost and the first such frost in the fall, is 120 days. Annual snowfall seldom tops ten feet.

But in June of 1816, after a long winter, a foot of snow fell, and strong winds created drifts three to five feet in height. No one had even seen anything like it. A little snow fell in July and August, and a severe frost struck on September 10th. No crops were harvested that year. The hay crop also failed, and most of Vermont's cattle starved to death as a result. Housewives swapped recipes for cooking porcupines, groundhogs, and raccoons (hint: use lots of onions). It is a fact that scores of thousands of Vermonters abandoned their farms in the Green Mountains and emigrated to Ohio and Indiana. Many from other New England states did likewise.

And yet, claim believers in witchcraft, all of this calamity was caused by a witch's curse: Elizabeth Leeds of Windsor was angry and vengeful.

It seems that in January 1816 Elizabeth begged her neighbors for some firewood. They selfishly and, it turned out, recklessly refused her. They should have known better, as Elizabeth already had a reputation of being a witch, and it is not a good idea to cross a witch. Elizabeth had been suspected, for example, of causing neighbors' cows to stop producing milk if she was refused some butter or cheese. Pigs would stop bearing piglets if Elizabeth was not gifted with a rasher or two of bacon. Yes, they should have known better than to deny the poor old woman some firewood in winter, but deny it they did.

In a cold fury, Elisabeth cursed the town, the whole state, and neighboring states as well for good measure. "You shall not see summer this year!" she screamed. And they didn't. Was the famine year a result of a witch's curse? Interestingly, climatologists never have agreed on exactly what caused such an abnormal year. Maybe there is something to a witch's curse.

The Thetford Horror

This story is difficult to document for several reasons. First and foremost is that no one is sure who, or what, severely mauled twelve dairy cows inside a barn near Thetford Center in the Connecticut Valley. There are three central theories concerning the culprit(s). One, favored by law enforcement, is that it was the work of Satanists, for there were indications of weird ritual practices. The dozen cows, their eyes torn out and their faces ripped open, were found, bloody and near death, arranged on the barn floor in a perfect circle. Their udders had been slashed apart by very sharp knives, or possibly very sharp teeth. Sixty other cows present were unharmed in their stalls. The satanic ritual theory explains the curtain of official secrecy surrounding the incident. Publicity, it was thought, might lead to copycat horrors, something no one wanted to encourage.

But, speaking of copycats, another theory involves a catamount, or mountain lion (also sometimes called a panther). Catamounts were (or are they still?) the top predators in Vermont. From pioneer days until the mid-nineteenth century, catamounts terrorized Vermont and its neighbors, killing sheep by the hundreds, cattle by the dozen, and even proved bold enough to attack men on horseback. As to mutilating their prey before finishing them off, toying with their prey is a characteristic of cats, as owners of housecats well know. Did a catamount savagely attack and mutilate the dairy cows? But how did it get into a locked barn and why would it arrange the dying animals in a circle?

Besides, the experts agree that the last catamount in Vermont was killed near Barnard in 1881. Stuffed, it now is on display in a glass case at the Vermont Historical Society Museum next door to the state capitol in Montpelier. And yet, people keep spotting the great cats (they can be four or five feet long not counting their long tails, and weigh over 100 pounds), at various locations around the state. Since once again Vermont hosts a large deer population (after deer nearly became extinct in the late nineteenth century), there would be ample prey to support a breeding population of mountain lions, should they recolonize the state from neighboring, documented populations.

A third theory, and a favorite of conspiracy buffs, is that the cattle were attacked by an unusually violent and uncharacteristically vicious pack of aliens from outer space. Given these choices, many Vermonters are rooting for the catamounts. The alternatives are scarier even than big cats on the prowl.

The Little Dog's Protective Spirit

One of the most charming ghosts, and most helpful, is that of a little Scots Terrier, once the pet of a family that still lives in White River Junction. "Cujo" was given that name because he was the opposite of Stephen King's villain in the novel of that name. This Cujo was diminutive, friendly, and thoroughly reliable. Believe it or not, Cujo was a good watchdog. He seemed always on the alert to any danger to his human family. His bright little eyes missed little and his hearing was legendary.

When at last Cujo went to dog heaven, as the parents told the children, it was decided to bury him in the backyard. Still wearing his red leather, chrome-studded collar, Cujo was laid to rest wrapped in the old bath towel that had lined his dog bed. Everyone missed him. Then, a few months after Cujo died, his ghost appeared to save the family from a near certain death. The family had retired for the night and, as was their custom, turned on the dishwasher just before going upstairs. The dishwasher churned away as everyone fell into a deep sleep. Then according to the fire marshall's subsequent investigation, the machine entered the drying cycle. The heating element somehow reached meltdown temperatures, setting fire to the surrounding wooden cabinets. A flash fire swept through the kitchen, spreading to other rooms.

Every family member later reported the same experience at approximately the same moment. Cujo, or rather Cujo's ghost, jumped up on their beds, barking his distinctively raspy short little bark and nuzzling their faces with his cold nose and quick tongue.

Everyone escaped the flames just in time, as they all rushed out into the hallway at the same time, and no precious seconds were wasted in awakening the others. Had they been alerted to mortal danger by the spirit of Cujo, or had they each separately dreamed of the brief reappearance of their pet? That quandary was resolved when one of the firefighters gave them something discovered in the ashes—a red leather, chrome-studded dog collar.

Lake Champlain Region

FRENCH EXPLORER SAMUEL DE CHAMPLAIN WAS THE FIRST EUROPEAN to visit what we now know as Vermont. He followed waterways south from Montreal, giving his name to the magnificent lake that is the focus of this region. This area stretches along Lake Champlain from the Canadian border to Fair Haven. It contains Vermont's largest city, Burlington, along with Winooski, Essex, and Vergennes.

The Confederate Ghosts of St. Albans

All right history buffs: What was the northernmost battle of the Civil War? Those answering "Gettysburg" get partial credit, for that mammoth struggle was the only major battle fought in the north, at least north of the Mason-Dixon line. But actually Vermont, and northern Vermont at that, was the scene of a Confederate raid, even if it doesn't quite merit the title battle.

It happened on October 19, 1864, only six months before General Lee surrendered his army to General Grant, effectively ending the War Between the States, as Southerners prefer to call it. Twenty-two Confederate soldiers, traveling in small groups and wearing civilian clothes over their gray uniforms, arrived in St. Albans over a period of several days, coming down from Canada, only fifteen

miles away. Combining bold action with careful planning, the Confederates entered all the banks in town simultaneously, killing one man and wounding several others. They fled northward with more than $200,000, setting fire to Sheldon Bridge behind them to slow pursuers. As they raced out of town, they threw off their civilian disguises, revealing their military uniforms beneath.

For more than a century after, the ghosts of the triumphant Confederates could be seen running gleefully from the banks, firing their revolvers in the air as they made good their escape. The phantoms of the undercover soldiers are seen but seldom these days on October 19th, the anniversary of their raid. Perhaps the shades of the Confederates have found peace at last, no longer needing to relive a rare moment of victory over the North after the "turning point" battles of Gettysburg and Vicksburg.

The ghosts of the Confederate raiders of St. Albans have every reason to joyously relive their stunning incursion into Vermont. They got away with it, and, at least briefly, carried the war deep into the north, striking terror and fear far beyond the battle lines.

Because by the time they crossed the border into Canada they were fully uniformed, officially enrolled Confederate soldiers, Canada accepted their claim that the St. Albans raid was a legitimate act of formal warfare. They were acquitted of robbery and murder charges. The British Empire favored the Confederacy during the Civil War but never openly supported it, proferring unofficial aid to their largest source of raw cotton for their mills.

There was such an international uproar over Canada's refusal to punish the perpetrators of the St. Albans raid that the Canadian Parliament voted $50,000 in gold for St. Albans as partial compensation. Should you encounter the shades of the Confederates fleeing St. Albans, stay out of their way. They are armed and they were the enemy.

The Black Snake Sails Again

The legend of the *Black Snake* still is told by oldtimers in the vicinity of St. Alban's Bay on Lake Champlain. And there have been sightings of this mysterious ship ever since her capture and destruction in 1808. Why does the *Black Snake* or rather its ghostly image, still sail on two centuries later?

The *Black Snake* was a very controversial vessel before her capture by federal officers so long ago, for she was built to smuggle Vermont products northward up Lake Champlain to Canada. In President Thomas Jefferson's opinion, *Black Snake* was an outlaw engaged in forbidden trade. To many Vermonters, the ship was a bold and profitable agent of Vermont enterprise and independent spirit.

Sightings of the phantom *Black Snake* may vary in details, but they generally agree on her appearance and behavior. She usually appears at dawn or dusk, often in fog, when visibility is limited. Early morning fishermen are among those who've witnessed the *Black Snake* sail by, a sight they'll never forget. The ship is entirely covered in black paint; even her canvas sails are dyed black—one reason for her name. A smuggling ship should either be too fast to catch or nearly impossible to see, or both, to avoid capture. Although Lake Champlain is pretty big as lakes go—120 miles long, and varying in width from one quarter of a mile to twelve miles— it would be difficult for a ship to speed away from pursuers and disappear like a ship on the vast ocean. And so *Black Snake* was designed to be almost invisible when she sailed the lake on moonless nights—entirely black and carrying no lights when on smuggling missions. The other reason for naming her *Black Snake?* Because black snakes are large, very aggressive snakes. Fortunately nonpoisonous, they have a nasty bite and have been known to drop out of trees onto people, giving them a huge fright as well as a few bite scars.

Although the phantom *Black Snake* doesn't "bite" (the ghost ship never shows any aggression toward those who see her), she certainly delivers a big scare just like her reptilian namesake. The all-black ghost ship appears suddenly out of the gloom. Her inky sails billow even in the absence of any wind. At first, the *Black Snake* seems to be headed on a collision course with the observers, but she veers off at the last minute, flashing by in complete silence. There is no one aboard the ghost ship. Curiously, she leaves no wake as she sails on in the direction of Canada.

Why were the owners and sailors of *Black Snake* regarded as heroes by many Vermonters? Landlocked Vermont in the early nineteenth century had no paved roads, and railroads had not yet been invented. Lake Champlain was comparable to a modern interstate highway connection toward Montreal, and most of northern Vermont's trade used the lake to sell products to Canada. When President Jefferson proclaimed an embargo that prohibited American trade with the British Empire, which included Canada, Vermont businesses were in danger of losing their best, and most accessible customers. Many in Vermont resorted to smuggling in order to pay their bills and feed their families, and so the sailors on smuggling ships like *Black Snake* were regarded as Vermont patriots rather than criminals. In capturing *Black Snake,* three federal agents were killed but only one smuggler was hanged. Others of *Black Snake's* crew were imprisoned but later pardoned by the governor of Vermont.

Sail on, *Black Snake*—symbol of Vermont's independent thinking and bold actions.

The Naked Swimmer's Ghost

One common element of most ghost stories is that the ghosts are fully clothed, or at least covered in the sheetlike white shrouds commonly used to cover corpses in the past. Naked ghosts are the exception, and a naked swimmer is a most unusual ghost indeed.

Although few have encountered the ghost of a naked swimmer recently, there is a local legend of such an apparition in Lake Champlain. This nude spirit is thought to be the ghost of Revolutionary War hero Richard Wallace. His is an interesting story.

It was late in the Fall of 1777. A British fleet controlled Lake Champlain. The American army was in trouble. Ethan Allen's brilliant capture of the mighty fortress of Fort Ticonderoga on May 10, 1775, had inspired the whole nation. Fort Ticonderoga commanded the narrow area where Lake George almost merges with Lake Champlain, essentially controlling the best route between Montreal and New York City. But the Americans were forced to evacuate Fort Ticonderoga on July 6, 1777, when British cannon made it open to attack. British forces also captured Mount Independence, an American fort constructed on the Vermont side of Lake Champlain just opposite Ticonderoga. But on October 17, 1777, the Americans retook their fort at Mount Independence, in large part thanks to the bravery of two men, Richard Wallace and Ephraim Webster. These two Vermonters volunteered to swim across Lake Champlain with important military dispatches. It was a night swim across two miles of ice cold water, zigzagging around British patrol boats that lay across their path. Wallace and Webster swam naked so that their clothes would not slow them down; the messages were tied to their foreheads in waterproof wrappings. The dispatches were delivered, and the Americans recaptured Mount Independence. It is said that Richard Wallace never fully recovered his health from this ordeal; perhaps this explains his ghostly swimming.

Those night fishermen who've caught a glimpse of the naked swimmer's ghost claim that they first heard the chattering of teeth before they actually saw the ghost. No wonder that the spirit's teeth are chattering or that the ghost is blue with cold! Should you spot the nude swimmer, perhaps you should salute an American hero as well as a unique ghost.

The Spirits of the Spiritualists

Queen City Park, on the southern edge of Burlington, boasts a fine bathing beach on Lake Champlain. And a large number of ghosts are said to hang out here, drawn by the history of this area, which once hosted a spiritualist campground famous throughout the country in the early twentieth century. Many citizens of Burlington believe that virtual conventions of spirits still assemble here on summer evenings, attempting to communicate with the living.

Early in the past century, there was great interest in spiritualism, a movement dedicated to the proposition that the living and the dead could, somehow, communicate with one another. The belief was widespread that the great void that separates heaven and earth, or perhaps in some cases, earth and the dreaded underworld, could be crossed with the aid of a medium. Mediums are those especially sensitive souls who possess the power to reach the spirits of the dead and transmit messages from the spirit world to living relatives and friends.

Spiritualism was quite fashionable, as many of the rich and famous expressed interest in it and had consulted mediums. Lectures on spiritualism were well received at prestigious universities and drew crowds to auditoriums and theaters. Everyone knew that Mrs. Abraham Lincoln regularly consulted mediums in her attempts to communicate with the martyred president. The famous author Sir Conan Doyle, creator of Sherlock Holmes, was fascinated with spiritualism and befriended famous mediums. The great magician,

Houdini, was very interested, if skeptical, in the possibility of contacting the spirit world.

The spiritualist campground at Queen City Park became a renowned center of lectures and appearances by famous mediums. Séances by the score were held every evening. The spirits, mostly unseen but sometimes heard, were said to make frequent contacts with the receptive living.

While the spiritualist campground long ago disappeared, the spirits have not. Many people have claimed that sundowns in summer along the lakeshore are marked by dozens of faintly phosphorescent figures drifting in from the lake. These spirits are peaceable enough, never deliberately frightening anyone. They seem content to wander around the former campground, perhaps searching for a receptive medium to transmit their messages to the world of the living.

Announcing a Death

There is a common type of ghost story in which a person is visited by the spirit of a loved one delivering a message—a message of danger or death. This appearance of a phantom, to say goodbye or announce the death of a third person, will later be seen to have occurred at the very moment of looming danger or death.

Such a story is told by the descendent of a prominent family in Burlington. The eldest son of a family of wealthy merchants had entered a career of service with the diplomatic corps. He and his wife and infant son were posted to an embassy in South America. At the time, there were no telegraph connections and mail took weeks to complete the journey (this was just before the Civil War).

Late one winter night, the mother of the diplomat was awakened to find her son standing in her room. He was dressed in his nightshirt and carrying a small bundle in his arms. The bundle was wrapped in a large cotton scarf that the lady had presented to her daughter-in-law as a bon voyage present. It had been hand-printed in a beautiful and unique design.

"James! Is that you? What are you doing back home?" she exclaimed. Without a word the figure slowly turned and revealed the lifeless body of his son swaddled in the scarf. As she watched, the figure of her son and his sad little burden seemed to fade away, gradually dissolving in a mist. Was it all a dream?

Weeks later, a letter arrived, reporting the death of her grandson from a tropical fever. The time and date of death coincided precisely with the ghostly appearance of her son in her bedroom. The letter advised that the infant's body had been embalmed and was being shipped home for burial in the family plot.

When, in due course, the coffin arrived, the child was found wrapped in the scarf the woman had seen in her dream—or was it a dream?

The Cold Lad

No one has seen this unusual ghost for many years, but there is a chance that he'll return. This particular ghost was "laid," as they used to say, by giving him a set of clothes, for he was very cold.

The story of the "cold lad," as he was called, goes back more than a century. The teenaged boy had been employed at a local inn as a kitchen helper and general errand boy. The owner of the inn had a notoriously bad temper and was quick with his fists. The lad was a good worker, one who took pride in doing a thorough job of cleaning the kitchen, scouring the pots and pans, and keeping the inn neat and immaculate.

But one winter day the teenager had left a particularly nasty pot soaking in the sink and forgot about it. The innkeeper, accustomed to everything being cleaned promptly, was furious. He angrily chastised the lad and, in a burst of temper, struck him a blow on the forehead, killing the lad instantly. Hoping to prevent the discovery of his crime, he stripped the body and secretly tossed it into Lake Champlain, tying weights to it to keep it on the bottom. Then the innkeeper burned all the lad's clothing and possessions. He announced that, following an argument, the lad had decided to move on.

The next spring, after the lake ice broke up, the inn's kitchen staff began to notice that during the night unfinished chores mysteriously would be completed. Pans left dirty would be shining bright. The floor would be freshly mopped, windows washed, and dishes neatly stacked in the cupboards.

Who was the volunteer clean-up helper? It was a puzzle, but at least it was a pleasant puzzle, making their jobs easier. As time went on, however, it became clear that their unseen helper not only wanted to do chores, but became annoyed if no work was left for the late night, unseen volunteer. If the kitchen staff left an immaculate kitchen, the next morning would find flour scattered on the floor, salt mixed in with sugar, or china broken in the sink.

Finally, the formerly unseen helper manifested himself. The missing teenager turned up, naked and shivering, blue with cold, sitting close by the kitchen fireplace. The staff began to call the apparition the "cold lad." Although nonthreatening, the nightly appearances of the cold lad were unnerving. What would persuade this ghost to leave? Obviously, he was very cold, being naked on cool Vermont nights. The kitchen staff hit on the idea of bringing warm clothing in appropriate sizes and leaving it in the kitchen. It worked. The set of clothes disappeared, and so did the cold lad. Will he come back when his clothing wears out? No one knows.

The Legendary Lake Champlain Monster

A huge monster lives in Lake Champlain. At least, that's what many people believe. Lake Champlain is big—120 miles long, varying in width from a quarter of a mile to twelve miles wide and reaching depths of 400 feet. Congress once voted to make Lake Champlain the sixth "Great Lake" (after Lakes Superior, Michigan, Huron, Erie, and Ontario, all of which, like Champlain eventually drain into the St. Lawrence River). The vote was rescinded after two months.

Two-thirds of Lake Champlain lies within Vermont; the rest is in New York State and Canada. The great French explorer, Samuel de Champlain, was the first European to see the lake he named for himself. He also was the first European to describe what the local Indians already knew and feared—the water serpent or monster that dwells in the depths of the lake.

Why are there so many stories of huge fish, enormous sea snakes, marine dinosaurs, and other fearsome monsters living in large lakes and rivers? One contributing factor is our fear of the unknown, our anxiety over what we cannot see readily or clearly. The depths can hide fierce predators—as *Jaws* dramatized so effectively.

The granddaddy (or is it grandmamma?) of all lake monsters is, of course, "Nessie," the elusive Loch Ness monster of Scotland. The legendary Nessie has been joined now by many others. Lake

Winnipeg, in Canada, supposedly hosts a monster called "Winnie." The Russians claim that the world's deepest lake, Lake Baikal, is inhabited by monsters. Early explorers claimed to have encounters with gigantic water serpents in Lakes Erie and Michigan. Big lakes and big monsters go hand in hand.

Lake Champlain's native monster has been nicknamed "Champ." As first described by Samuel de Champlain, Champ is a serpentine creature twenty feet long, as thick as a barrel, and with a head like a horse. More recent sightings liken Champ to a long-necked, dinosaurlike predator with paddlelike fins and dark, scaly skin, rather like a cousin of Nessie.

Nessie and Champ have more in common than just their general appearance. Their homes are very similar. Both Lake Champlain and Loch Ness are very deep freshwater bodies connected to the sea. Both occupy part of enormous natural trenches in the earth's crust—the result of titanic forces in the crust that created parallel fractures across mountainous terrain. Loch Ness is in the "Great Glen" (valley) that nearly splits Scotland from east to west. Lake Champlain, Lake George, and the Hudson Valley are all part of a huge lowland trench connecting Montreal and New York City.

Is Champ real? Does Nessie exist? There are no clear, authenticated photos of either creature, at least pictures that could not have been faked, or which might just show ripples in the water from boat wakes. Serious scientific expeditions, particularly in Loch Ness, have failed to prove that the supposed monsters really exist. On the other hand, there is no proof that such creatures could not be lurking in the depths.

Marine biologists say that the question is not, "Is there a monster?" but, "Could there be such a monster?" It comes down to food. A breeding population of large carnivores would require a large food base of fish. Some scientists claim that, yes, there are enough salmon, bass, trout, and eels to supports large meat-eating creatures. Others point out that if Champ (and Nessie) are cold-blooded animals like dinosaurs are assumed to have been, they could, like alligators, live months between meals.

Although Champ has been accused of deliberately upsetting small boats, there is no record of the monster actually attacking people. As a result, Champ generally is viewed as relatively harmless, a kind of mascot for the tourist industry in the area, again, similar to

Nessie. Several towns along the lakeshore have declared themselves safe havens for Champ, promising not to harass him or attempt to capture him. One can hope that Champ watches TV or reads the local papers so that he understands this "live and let live" attitude. If you venture out on Lake Champlain, or visit its lovely beaches, remember to keep your camera handy. You might get lucky.

The Great White Horse of Winooski

The handsome white stallion races along the lush meadows that lie next to the Winooski River north of Burlington. Head held high, his white mane rippling in the wind, the horse is the very picture of vigor, independence, and adventure. Many have caught a glimpse of the powerful stallion, running free on misty mornings through the Winooski Valley Park. Should anyone attempt to approach the magnificent animal, however, it seems to evaporate before their eyes, for they have seen a ghost. Not just any ghost, for many are convinced that the phantom horse is the spirit of Ethan Allen, Vermont's most famous son.

Ethan Allen, whose restored homestead sits atop a low bluff overlooking the riverside meadows along the Winooski, was a complex and controversial man. Ethan was a courageous patriot, a flamboyant military leader, a prisoner of war, a land speculator, a farmer, a highly independent thinker, a renowned storyteller, and, just possibly, a drunk, a traitor, and a bully.

One thing about him on which all historians can agree, however, is that there would not be a state of Vermont without his determined leadership. Although his great popularity and charismatic personality surely could have made him governor of the state he founded, Ethan never held elected office. Strongly opposed to organized religion, he refused to take an oath on a Bible, effectively banning him from public office. He was very influential in the government of the free and independent Republic of Vermont, which lasted from 1776 until admission to the Union on March 4, 1791, and in the new state as well.

Ethan Allen wrote his own "bible," a book called *Reason the Only Oracle of Man.* He was a deist—that is, he believed in God but did not accept any organized religion. Apparently he believed in reincarnation, for he often told friends that he intended to return after death in the form of "a great white horse." There is no way to know if he was serious or just having a good joke on his friends. Ethan was a great storyteller and was known to stretch the truth a bit when telling tales in a friendly tavern.

He liked to rewrite history in the cause of making a story more entertaining. An example is his published version of the capture of Fort Ticonderoga. Allen and eighty-three of his Green Mountain Boys took this powerful and awesome fort from the sleeping British garrison on May 10, 1775. The Americans captured 150 cannon, which George Washington put to good use later. The story was that Ethan Allen knocked at Ticonderoga's gate late that night and demanded the fort's surrender. "By what right do you demand surrender?" asked the lone sentry on duty. "In the name of the Great Jehovah and the Continental Congress!" Allen later wrote. An eyewitness, however, claimed that what Ethan Allen really said was, "Come out of there you old rat and show us where you keep the rum!"

Still, Ethan Allen's tendency to brag about his great accomplishments and his known fondness for strong drink cannot detract from his major contribution to American independence. It would be entirely appropriate if indeed his fiercely independent spirit lives on as a great white horse—running joyously free near the house in which he died after a remarkable career as a soldier patriot. As George Washington observed of Ethan Allen, there was "an original something in him that commands admiration."

The Pirate Treasure of Mallets Bay

Pirate treasure in Vermont? It sounds extremely unlikely. After all, Vermont is the only New England state that does not have an ocean shoreline. Nonetheless, there long have been rumors of buried pirate treasure, complete with guardian ghost, in the vicinity of Mallets Bay, directly north of Burlington on Lake Champlain.

As is common with old legends, there seems to be several different versions of the story of Captain Mallet's treasure. There isn't even any agreement on the pirate's name, if indeed he was a pirate. Vermont's own version of Captain Kidd, Captain Mallet's (or is it Mallett?) first name is variously given as Stephen, or Pierre, or Jean-Pierre. There seems to be general agreement that he was a Frenchman.

According to some stories, Mallet was a kind of leftover from the days when this whole area was claimed by France, on the strength of Samuel de Champlain's explorations. He may simply have been a wealthy landowner who stashed his gold in a buried chest to keep English hands off it.

Or, in a more romantic version, Captain Mallet was a successful pirate who retired to Vermont, far from the saltwater on which he robbed ships of all nations. An alternative theory is that the Emperor Napoleon had entrusted Mallet with the payroll, all in gold, for all French officials and soldiers in far-off Louisiana. Mallet was supposed to deliver this gold to New Orleans when it was still French, but the captain decided to keep the money for himself and hide out in Vermont instead.

So, one way or another, Captain Mallet had a large chest of gold, which, in true pirate fashion, he buried. In keeping with the tradition of buried pirate loot, Mallet is supposed to have murdered an associate, placing his corpse atop the treasure. The ghost is then supposed to have protected the treasure for eternity.

A gruesome ghost is alleged to rise up, bloody cutlass in hand, to scare off anyone who might come too close to the Captain Mallet's treasure. The location of the ghost and treasure, however, is uncertain, as is Mallet's identity and past. Some say the ghost patrols Mallets Head, while others place it on Coate's Island in Mallets Bay, so you have your choice of haunted treasure sites. Good hunting, but watch out for the cutlass-waving ghost.

The Doctor Is In

Most doctors today just don't make house calls, unless of course one happens to be sharing rooms with a doctor—a doctor who happens to be a ghost.

Actually, the ghost in question isn't, or rather wasn't, quite a doctor. He was a medical student at the University of Vermont, and the pressures of his impending final exams led to his suicide, which led to his present ghostly status.

The ghost of the doctor, or almost doctor in this case, is said to haunt a large old house near the university campus in Burlington. From the phantom's viewpoint, he practices on the students now occupying rooms where he lived. And died.

Medical schools are pressure chambers. The standards are very high, the demands unrelenting, and the stakes high. The story is that, in the late 1950s, a medical student whom we'll call Jack Broward, cracked under the pressure. Studying for final exams proved too much for him. Jack hanged himself from a roof support in the attic of his rooming house. Although he left no note, the police were satisfied that it was a suicide, carried out under extreme mental and emotional stress. Case closed.

Jack's body was hardly in his grave when students in his old rooming house began to dream that a doctor was examining them as they slept. They had vague memories of a doctor, complete in white lab coat, stethoscope and kindly, concerned expression, bending over them. And then the "prescriptions" began to appear—not real prescriptions, for the phantom "doctor" had no intention of breaking the law and getting his "patients" in trouble by their trying to have prescriptions filled that were not written by a licensed doctor. "Doctor Jack," as the ghost came to be called, would leave notes at the bedside, offering a diagnosis and a recommendation on over-the-counter medications that would help. If the phantom physician detected a serious health problem, the bedside note would recommend the appropriate specialist associated with the medical school.

The "patients" weren't sure what to do with this supernatural HMO. The medical diagnoses usually proved correct when a live doctor was consulted, and the "prescriptions" and "referrals" appropriate. No harm and much good resulted from the ghost's well-intentioned exams. Most beneficiaries of Dr. Jack calmly accepted the idea that they were being visited by an unobtrusive phantom. Doctor Jack's exams and prescriptions seem to be becoming less frequent now. Has the phantom physician reached retirement age? Or has he at last moved on to the spirit world?

Cleopatra's Curse

In the 1840s, there was a fad for classical names, and so a nice Vermont farm girl found herself labeled Cleopatra after the scheming, ill-fated Queen of Egypt. This Vermont Cleopatra, like her namesake, was beautiful, clever, and, it turned out, ill-fated as well.

Cleo married a shrewd livestock trader and real estate speculator who made a fortune selling Vermont beef to the Union army during the Civil War. After the war, he built a fabulous mansion on Isle la Motte, set amongst apple orchards on the banks of Lake Champlain. Life was good.

Cleo and her husband produced only one child—a late life surprise but a very welcome one. Their daughter, Jenny, inherited her mother's beauty but not her brains. She married an ambitious, not very smart, and, shall we say, ethically challenged young man, Adam Schnell. Schnell, whose name meant "quick" in German, wasn't quick in the area of common sense. He invested unwisely in the stock market, losing his and Jenny's money. He asked his wealthy widowed mother-in-law, with whom the couple lived in Cleo's mansion, for a loan. He got it. His next money-making scheme was to invest in a company drilling for oil—in Vermont. After drilling an exceedingly expensive hole through solid Vermont granite, they struck saltwater and went bankrupt. Adam asked Cleo for another loan. She refused on the grounds that, in her words, "he hasn't the brains of a flea." Her son-in-law decided that his wife's inheritance as sole heir was his only hope. There was the little problem that Cleo was still alive, very healthy, and very determined that Adam Schnell would not see any money in her lifetime.

And so Adam decided to poison the old lady, slowly, carefully, making it look like a lingering illness rather than a suspiciously sudden death. But before her agonizing death, Cleo figured out what was happening. "You and yours will never prosper," she said as she cursed him, "and your bloodline will end at the third generation."

After Cleo was buried under a suitably Egyptian-looking obelisk, Adam started investing his wife's substantial inheritance. Having concluded that Vermont oil wells were a tad risky, Adam put most of their money in conservative government bonds. Unfortunately, they were bonds issued by the Imperial Russian government, which ceased to exist in 1917, rendering them valueless.

Adam died a bitter and much poorer man in 1920, leaving behind Adam Junior as the sole heir to what was left of Grandma Cleo's money. Junior wisely avoided foreign bonds, instead investing heavily in the stock market. The great crash of October 1929 wiped him out, contributing to his suicide. His only offspring, a childless daughter with some of her great-grandmother's brains, became an archeologist. On a dig in Egypt, she was fatally bitten by an asp, the same type of poisonous snake that the original Cleopatra had used to commit suicide. The Schnell bloodline indeed had died out in the third generation. Was the unhappy history of Adam Schnell's descendents a string of coincidences or the result of Cleopatra's (the Vermont one's) curse?

The Case of the Flattened Flatlander

In Vermont, the term "flatlander," as applied to a person, definitely is not intended as a compliment. As anyone who has ever seen Vermont knows, it is anything but flat. The Green Mountain State is as accurate a nickname for a state as they come. Thus, a flatlander is by definition an outsider. But Vermonters have extended the definition of flatlander to include both outsiders and Vermonters who are: (a) somewhat deficient in functioning brain cells; (b) seldom able to appreciate true beauty, i.e., Vermont, when they see it; (c) downright greedy; (d) short-sighted; and (e) insensitive to the environment; or (f) all of the above ("f" is the correct answer in most cases).

There is a war going on in Vermont. It is not always noisy, but it is continuing. It seldom produces dead bodies to be shown on the evening news, for the casualties are mostly the losses of places of beauty. It is the war between developers and preservationists, the war for the future of Vermont.

There is the matter of geography. Vermont is stunningly, absolutely beautiful. It also is handy to hoards of flatlanders who would like to buy their own piece of this beauty. Understandable. Unfortunately, the realization that very large numbers of new arrivals can threaten the quality of life that first attracted them can come slowly to the environmentally brain-dead, or flatlanders, as Vermonters might call them.

Near South Burlington, the war between developers and preservationists did produce a dead body. The mysterious case of the flattened flatlander was never solved. Many believe that it involves supernatural forces protecting the future of Vermont.

Vermont's "godfather," Ethan Allen, famously said, "The gods of the valleys are not the gods of the hills." He wouldn't further explain this cryptic remark, but most Vermonters understand his point. Vermonters, or at least most of them, have a different perspective on life than do flatlanders. Even though there is much money to be made in the process, most Vermonters do not wish to experience the large-scale developments that characterize, say, New Jersey or Long Island.

It was at a construction site for a large shopping center that the flatlander got flattened. He was an out-of-state developer who, literally, got flattened—in this case by a large diesel Caterpillar bulldozer. It happened late at night within a fenced and locked area used for onsite equipment storage. Unaccountably (there were no keys for the dozer at the site), the machine ran over the man, breaking every bone, and terminating, at least for him, a lot of future development plans. No one ever was charged in this death. Was the case of the flattened flatlander just an urban legend? Or did the spirits intervene to keep the Green Mountain State green?

The Devil Dogs of Vergennes

The recently widowed parishioner came to her priest with a unique problem. She was being harassed, she claimed, by devil dogs, the canine servants of Satan. She swore that she knew of nothing that would attract the special attention of the lord of the underworld to her house. The hounds from hell appeared in her kitchen every night, forcing the terrified old woman to retreat behind the locked door of her bedroom.

Her house was an old one, near the center of one of America's oldest incorporated towns. Was it possible that the Devil had sent his minions to that house seeking the soul of some previous tenant? After all, Vergennes once had been known, at least to the British, as the Devil's Workshop. During the War of 1812, Vergennes foundries had cast 177 tons of cannon balls. Was the Devil in league with the British? Well, some patriotic Americans might have thought so, but did the Devil really take sides?

For whatever reason, the old woman was being harassed by devil dogs, or so she claimed. Her priest was somewhat skeptical of the supernatural, but the poor woman's terror seemed real enough. He agreed to come to her house and confront the devil dogs.

Armored with crucifix, Bible, and a small bottle of holy water, the priest showed up that evening at the woman's house. They agreed that she would lock herself in her bedroom while the priest stayed in the kitchen. Not quite knowing what to do, and not at all sure that there actually were material manifestations of the evil one, he sprinkled holy water around the chair he was to occupy. He opened his Bible and began to read.

The hours dragged by and he had just begun to nod off when a puppy appeared—but how, as all the doors had been carefully locked? Wagging its tail, the apparently friendly little dog approached as if to nuzzle the priest. Abruptly, it stopped, straining as though held back by an unseen leash. The formerly innocent looking puppy transformed into a snarling beast, its fangs dripping hot saliva mixed with blood. The priest shivered involuntarily. Despite frantic lunging, the dog never reached him. It could not penetrate the protective circle of holy water to the great relief of the priest. The frustrated beast then turned on its tail, which it devoured, finally consuming itself in a mist of blood.

Badly shaken, the priest reported all of this to the owner of the cursed house, agreeing to return the next evening. That night started out as a repeat of the first, until a large powerful looking Doberman suddenly materialized. Growling ominously, it leaped toward the priest, only to stop in midair as the priest held forth his crucifix. Yelping as though in pain, the Doberman lept into the roaring fire on the hearth and was gone. The priest shuddered at the thought of what the next night would bring, but he pledged to his parishioner that he would come back.

Assuming that an even more fearsome dog would appear that evening, the priest made careful preparations. He brought with him his crucifix, Bible, and holy water and wore his full vestments as though about to say mass. And he brought along a few pounds of fresh steak from the butcher shop.

That third and most awesome devilish apparition was a massive, two-headed hound, each head featuring a mouthful of razor-sharp teeth. The monster's red-hot breath evaporated the drops of holy water surrounding his chair, set fire to the Bible, and melted the silver crucifix. Satan had sent his most aggressive demon dog to attack the priest. Then the priest tossed huge raw steaks to each of the fiend's gaping jaws. The demon, thinking that this was a pathetic attempt to bribe it, snapped up the offerings. Then an unexpected, searing pain struck the devil dog. Howling in anguish, the beast began to burn from the inside out. The steaks had concealed vials of holy water, which as the massive teeth pulverized the thin glass, poured down the twin throats of the monster with the same effect as gasoline on a fire. The devil dog was destroyed. Satan's minions never returned to that house.

Who Is Buried in Ethan Allen's Grave?

Vermont's real founder and most important historical figure is buried at Greenmount Cemetery on Colchester Avenue in Burlington. Or is he? Everyone certainly assumed so, reassured by a beautiful statue of Ethan Allen, eight-feet tall, carved of Cararra marble and placed on a forty-two-foot granite shaft resting on an eight-foot granite base. The statue, in a typically theatrical and aggressive pose, is entitled "Ticonderoga" in commemoration of Allen's memorable victory in the American Revolution. All of this is surrounded by a cast-iron fence made to look like muskets and cannon.

There is only one small problem. When archeologists dug into Allen's nearby gravesite, as recorded on the cemetery plot map, they found nothing. No coffin, no bones, no trace at all of the famous war hero and leader. Where was he? What happened?

First, the official version. There had been an error in the cemetery records. Allen actually was buried about forty feet from the site first identified as his grave. He was there, almost certainly. Almost? Well, after all these years (he died on February 13, 1789), there is not much left that is identifiable. Now for the conspiracy version. Allen's family were following his last wishes when they deliberately mislabeled his last resting place. Supposedly, Allen feared that grave robbers would dig up his corpse and sell it for medical research. Or in some versions, Ethan Allen was concerned that jealous enemies would dig him up and desecrate his body in witchcraft ceremonies. Or, (a personal favorite of Ethan Allen admirers) maybe he didn't want to be buried at all in a public cemetery and was secretly interred elsewhere, where he wouldn't be surrounded by believers in organized religion. He was a free thinker who once wrote his own "bible," a statement of his personal philosophy.

So where are Ethan Allen's bones? It seems that, in death as in life, he remains controversial, an enigma to both friend and foe. One can hope that his body never became the basis for witchcraft as some believe.

Northeast Kingdom

THE NORTHEAST CORNER OF VERMONT, NORTH OF MCINDOE FALLS ON the Connecticut River and, essentially, east of Interstate 91, was given the name "Northeast Kingdom" about seventy-five years ago in recognition of its unique character. With only one important town, St. Johnsbury, this is a land of dense forests, few people, and more than a few reports of Bigfoot sightings. The pristine lakes, ponds, and rivers help make this region a favorite with outdoor camping enthusiasts and hunters and fishermen.

The Mysterious End of Arcadia Retreat

Arcadia is a classical place name—a reference to a pleasant countryside in Greece whose name has become synonymous with tranquil rural beauty and quiet enjoyment of solitude and the simple life. Most of Vermont would fit that description, especially the "Northeast Kingdom." Near the shores of Lake Willoughby lie the remains of the stone foundations of Arcadia Retreat, once a fashionable and exclusive resort. Arcadia Retreat had a brief, unhappy existence, a sparkling gem of an elite resort that suddenly and mysteriously was abandoned. The handsome hotel, lavishly furnished and outfitted with the finest of every comfort and convenience for the pleasure of its wealthy guests, went out of business literally overnight around 1900. No one ever returned to claim the furnishings and attempt the sale of the resort. Gradually, local people helped themselves to beds, drapes, kitchen equipment, and the like. The empty shell finally burned down in the 1920s, leaving little trace of the once fabled retreat.

There were persistent rumors that Arcadia Retreat's owners, staff, and guests were forced to flee in fear of their lives because the hotel was haunted—completely, violently, and hopelessly haunted. Sadly, the builders of Arcadia Retreat had been warned not to build on the spot, as it contained a large Indian burial ground. The spirits of the dead, the newcomers were advised, would seek revenge on anyone who desecrated their last resting place.

Legend had it that an entire army of Indian warriors had been buried at the site of a mighty battle between the great Iroquois and Algonquin nations who had contended for these lands long ago. Their spirits were restive, having been slain in battle. No sooner had ground been broken for the new resort than accidents began to plague the workers. A roofer fell to his death on the stone patio below. A well digger died when the sides of the well collapsed, burying him alive. Several laborers died of mysterious, paralyzing illnesses after digging the foundations.

The tragedies increased after the grand opening. A honeymooning couple jumped, hand in hand, from the top of the tower, dying instantly. The head chef poisoned two of his staff, then shot himself. A chambermaid hanged herself in her attic room. Four young children drowned in the hotel pool all on one day. That same evening, about twenty hotel guests ran hysterically through the lobby, screaming that they were being chased by tomahawk-wielding ghostly warriors. Arcadia Retreat was hastily abandoned by its terrified staff and guests. No one ever again spent the night there until it was consumed by fire many years later. The site was never rebuilt, for obvious reasons. The vengeful ghosts of slain warriors are back in quiet repose. Until the next time their long sleep is disturbed, that is.

Exorcizing a Witch

Many years ago a farm family had to rid themselves, and their neighbors, of a witch. It happened in the tiny village of Westmore on Lake Willoughby, a hard place to make a living farming (not that any place in the Green Mountain State could be called easy living). Times were tough, and on the Layton farm, things were getting mighty desperate. Daisy, their cow, had given no milk for seven days in a row, yet usually she was a good milk producer. The hens had laid no eggs, another disaster.

The Layton's neighbors all had similar complaints about a streak of bad luck. One's orchard had had a mysterious disappearance of ripe apples from the tree. Another neighbor's prize pig had lost weight suddenly, despite its huge appetite. The family suspected old Granny Hawkins, a long-time neighbor whose behavior had changed abruptly. Could Granny have become a witch?

The father and his eldest son determined to investigate. One evening they crept up to Granny's house and peered in the kitchen window. They could hardly believe their eyes. Granny Hawkins had drawn a pentagram on the floor, the five points marked by candles. Mumbling some arcane incantations, she removed a scarf from around her neck, draped it over a rope, and squeezed a pail of fresh milk from the scarf. Next, she placed the scarf over a shallow bowl, then whisked it away, revealing a mound of butter. The bewitched scarf was then used to magically produce cheese, a basket of eggs, a bushel of ripe apples, and even a side of bacon.

"Well, now we know what happened to Daisy's milk and our hen's eggs!" grumbled the farmer as they headed home. "But I know how to deal with a witch." Dan Layton cut the bark off one part of the trunk of a living pine tree. On the fresh white wood, he used charcoal to draw the image of Granny Hawkins, carefully labeling the image with her name. He then melted a silver coin into a bullet mold. Next, the silver bullet was fired into the tree trunk portrait. "We must never cut down that tree," he advised his family, "for it now contains all that was evil about Granny Hawkins."

Sure enough, Granny, complaining of a sharp pain in her chest, once again was the sweet old lady she had been before she was bewitched by the Devil. The neighborhood's cows, hens, apple trees, and hogs all resumed normal production and weight. The grateful neighbors took care to graciously share their produce with poor old Granny. Normal life returned and that pine tree never was cut down.

The UFO and the Campers

Vermont's "Northeast Kingdom" is a vacationer's wonderland of mountains, forests, lakes, and whitewater, tumbling streams—a near-pristine wilderness. Vermont's northeastern-most county, Essex, contains only about 6,500 permanent residents. Brighton State Park, near beautiful Island Pond, is one of many perfect spots for family camping. It was there that a vacationing family from Boston had an encounter with a UFO and its crew, or so they believe. They've shared their experience only with close friends, and only on the grounds of anonymity.

For one thing, the family of four—we'll call them the Bentleys— are not absolutely certain that any of this actually happened. It could have been all a dream, although both parents and their son and daughter all had the exact same dream, which would seem unlikely. Also, the family's German Shepherd mix, Fritz, was nearly catatonic for a few days following their possible encounter with the unknown, and unknowable.

The Bentleys were "pushing the season," deciding to camp out in northern Vermont in early May, when nights still are quite cold. As a result, they had the area to themselves, with no other campers in sight. As they toasted marshmallows over the campfire after a hearty meal of roasted hot dogs, an odd, cigar-shaped craft appeared directly over their campsite. It hovered like a large helicopter, but there was a distinct lack of the clattering sound of a helicopter. Suddenly, a brilliant white light was beamed on them from above. They each felt immobilized, as though drugged. Then, each in turn, and including Fritz, was enveloped in a glowing cylinder for a few moments, during which they felt a mild euphoria. They later concluded that they had been subjected to some kind of non-invasive total body and mind scan—a kind of thorough examination at the hands of the unseen crew of the space craft.

The family members remembered only that the strange craft abruptly rose vertically, following their "exams," then accelerated rapidly as it flew directly north and out of sight. Family members quickly came out of their near-trance, but their dog remained in a motionless state all night long and resumed his normal life only after a few more days of dazed lethargy.

The Bentleys decided that a UFO visiting earth had selected them for some sort of scientific study because they were so isolated from other people in that wilderness campground area. Since their encounter, the Bentleys have restricted their camping to busy, commercial campgrounds and in high season. No more solitude for them.

Slow Pierre's Guardian Spirit

Only a few people around St. Johnsbury still remember the tale of "Slow Pierre's" guardian spirit, for it happened long ago. Curiously, it is a ghost story in which the ghost, if that is what it was, made only one appearance.

In the early days of railroading switches were thrown by hand, on the spot, not operated remotely as today. Moving the heavy steel rails manually was a tough job—one that required brawny muscles together with a strong sense of responsibility, for timely switching on the line could either prevent an accident, or cause one if not done precisely on schedule. At isolated, rural switching points, the job of switchman was a combination of boredom most of the day, but being right on time those moments that really counted.

Some miles north of St. Johnsbury was a most critical switching point, a switch that would divert a train onto a lightly used line toward a logging camp or keep it on the main line toward St. Johnsbury. The schedule called for a slow-moving freight train to enter the branch line toward the logging camp at 9:25 p.m. Immediately after this freight crossed the switch, it must be thrown back into the main line position to accommodate the fast passenger train running between Montreal and Boston, due there at 9:35. Were the switch not returned promptly to the main line position, the "Montreal Flyer," as it was known, could enter the branch line and rear-end the slower freight.

"Slow Pierre" as he was known, was slightly mentally handicapped but was extremely conscientious about his duties. He was proud of being trusted to move the switch every evening and didn't mind the hours of boredom between switching chores. As soon as the freight had negotiated the switch toward the logging camp, Pierre would return the switch to its normal main-line position, then stand by the switch holding a lantern steadily aloft to reassure the swiftly approaching Flyer that it was clear. If the switch could not be moved in time, Pierre was to swing the lantern back and forth rapidly, signaling an emergency stop.

One winter morning, the railroad's section supervisor came by with Pierre's pay envelope, only to find the loyal switchman dead in his little shack by the switch. A doctor estimated that Slow Pierre had suddenly died twenty-four hours before his body was discovered. But why didn't the Montreal Flyer follow the freight onto the branch line? On being questioned, the Flyer's engineer said that the steady lantern had, as usual, illuminated Slow Pierre's smiling face as he signaled that all was well, that the switch had been thrown for the flyer. It was not possible, but it happened, and the swift passenger train was safely routed on the main line. Had Slow Pierre's loyalty and conscientious pride in his trust somehow motivated his spirit to do his vital job one more time? The ghost of Slow Pierre never appeared again, once a living replacement took over as switchman. Slow Pierre had been faithful even in death.

The Sabbath Gambler

The Puritans, who were so important in settling much of New England, definitely did not believe in gambling. Actually, the Puritans had a rather long list of things of which they did not approve. Someone once defined a Puritan as someone who lived in fear that, somewhere, somehow, somebody was having fun.

But gambling on cards was near the top of the list, as was not keeping the Sabbath. An old legend in St. Johnsbury is that a local merchant and landowner, a habitual gambler, not only broke the ban on gambling and card playing, but broke it on a Sabbath.

Andy Richardson was a compulsive gambler. He'd bet on anything, but preferred a game of cards. In common with other gambling addicts, Andy would foolishly insist on another game, and then another, when his luck was running bad. Driven by an almost insane need to recoup his losses, Andy would keep raising the stakes as his money flowed across the card table to his opponents.

Although he was a shrewd, successful businessman and had inherited several farms and a maple syrup and candy factory, Andy's gambling began to decimate his fortune. In the staid St. Johnsbury of a century and a half ago, Andy earned a notorious reputation. Friends and neighbors who used to enjoy a friendly game at the card table with modest stakes stopped playing with Andy as his tantrums when losing began to frighten them. Andy's uncle, a minister in the Congregational Church, visited him to implore him to stop gambling, most especially on the Sabbath.

This visit, which took place on a Sabbath, only served to infuriate Andy. "I'll gamble how and when I please!" he shouted as he saw his uncle to the door. His usual card-playing buddies refused him a game, several citing the Sabbath as their excuse. Even his butler and cook, normally eager to please the boss, declined his invitation to a game.

"Damn!" he exclaimed. "Will no one join me in a game?" There was a knock at the door. A tall stranger, dressed all in black, stood on the threshold. "I'd like a game or two," he said, "but only for high stakes." "Done!" said his host, leading him to the card room and shutting the door.

Soon the servants were hearing Andy loudly cursing his bad luck as hand after hand went against him. The shouting grew louder and more abusive. Finally, Andy was heard to yell, "Then take my soul, damn you!" At that, there was a loud crash. On entering the card room, the servants found Andy face down on the floor, dead of a stroke, a hideous expression on his face. There was no sign of the stranger. Had Andy finally found a high-stakes player willing to gamble on the Sabbath? Had he wagered his soul to the Devil?

Outsmarting a Ghost

In the little town of Lyndon, some old-timers enjoy retelling the story of how a vindictive ghost was outsmarted. Outsmarted by a shrewd "Yankee trader," a special breed of crafty merchant whose bargaining skills are among the world's finest.

It happened that a country store was for sale. The country store had no close-by competitors, was well located at a crossroads, and occupied a sizeable and soundly built structure. The price was reasonable. Everything pointed to a golden opportunity, which made the prospective buyer, an experienced trader, ask more probing questions. Just why was it such an irresistible deal? Something must be wrong somewhere.

In due course, the trader, one Bill Watson, learned about one little problem. The store was haunted. Furthermore, it was haunted by a particularly vengeful ghost, that of a boy of twelve.

The story was that this boy had been orphaned when his parents died in a flood, leaving him the sole heir to their prosperous country store. The boy's uncle was to act as his guardian and operate the store until the boy was an adult, placing all the profits in trust for his nephew. But the uncle was very poor and very ruthless, a combination that proved fatal to the young boy. Desiring to keep the store for himself, the uncle poisoned his nephew. Secretly burying the body nearby, the uncle told everyone that the lad had run away to join the gold rush to California, and that he, the uncle, was to run the store in his absence. This deception worked well enough, and the uncle and his business prospered.

Until, that is, the wicked uncle was killed by a bolt of lightning, a bolt from a clear blue sky on the first anniversary of the boy's disappearance. After that, the country store passed through the hands of several storekeepers, each of whom left in a hurry after being terrorized by the boy's ghost.

Now Bill Watson figured that everyone had a price and that he could negotiate with the best, or the worst. He hired a gypsy to hold a séance and summon forth the boy's ghost. The spirit duly appeared. What did the ghost want in order to stop haunting the store? The room shook with the pent-up rage of the ghost. "I demand a sacrifice—an unholy sacrifice to placate my spirit. I demand a body and soul thrown into a bonfire in front of my store!" screamed the apparition.

"It's a deal," was Bill's quick reply, much to the horror of the gypsy medium. The bonfire was built, and into it Bill tossed the body of a piglet and the sole of a shoe. Outsmarted, the vengeful ghost crept off, vowing never again to bargain with a Yankee trader.

A Death Foretold

A family in St. Johnsbury tells the story of how a young woman's death was foretold by the ghost of her own mother. Eileen was a beautiful young woman, apparently in excellent health and looking forward to starting college in a few months.

Eileen's mother had died in childbirth, so that Eileen knew her only from a handful of photographs. She always wondered what her mother had been like and was reassured by her father that her mother had been a sweet and loving person, who had been looking forward to rearing the child she was carrying. Happily for everyone, Eileen's stepmother provided all the loving care a child would wish for. Still, Eileen often expressed regret at having no memories of her birth mother.

Just after retiring to bed one evening, Eileen awoke to find every light shining in her room. She was sure she had turned out all the lights, but did so again, and fell asleep. At about two in the morning, Eileen awoke, again finding all the lights on. This time, the figure of her mother, recognizable from her photos, stood by her bed. The ghost gently told Eileen that she should have no fear, that her mother was quite happy to see her, and that the two would be reunited by noon of the same day. The phantom then evaporated before Eileen's eyes.

A very thoughtful girl stayed in her room by herself way past breakfast. When at last she came downstairs, she handed her stepmother a sealed envelope, instructing her to give it to Eileen's father in the event of her sudden death. Eileen then called the parish priest and asked if he could visit her as soon as possible. Her private meeting with the priest had just concluded when, as the clock began chiming noon, Eileen collapsed and died.

In her final letter to her father, Eileen described her experience and asked that she be buried next to her mother. At long last, she would get to know her.

The Devil's Tree

There is a legend in the vicinity of Island Pond that is so old that few still remember it. The Devil's Tree, as the locals called it, is no more, nor, for that matter, is the house on whose lawn it once stood. The Devil's Tree was an ancient oak, nearly split in two by a long ago lightning strike. A few branches still managed to sprout green every spring. The fact that the immense old tree had survived a lightning strike contributed to its reputation as an unusual specimen. The main reason for its ominous name, however, was the rumor that an Indian massacre had occurred beneath its branches. Also, it was a fact that a previous owner of the house nearby had been found hanging from its limb one summer morning. It had never been determined whether this was a suicide or murder.

The house at the Devil's Tree was purchased by a Boston businessman who used it only for the summer months. The year-round caretaker was a local man named Jack Nolan, who earned an unsavory reputation in the neighborhood. In the absence of the owner, Jack strode arrogantly around the property, accompanied by a large, aggressive dog. There were rumors of satanic ceremonies held at the house in the absence of the owner.

Then one day, Nolan was gone. The house owner arrived to find the house wide open and ransacked. Sterling silverware and jewelry were missing. A manhunt failed to turn up Jack Nolan. Neighbors began complaining of loud moans and cries seeming to come from the Devil's Tree. Was the tree truly haunted? Had Jack Nolan entered into a pact with the Devil?

The owner of the house decided to have the Devil's Tree cut down. As no local workmen would go near the tree with an evil reputation, a team of tree surgeons was brought in all the way from Boston. When the massive old tree was cut down, they made a grisly discovery. The lightning-seared and blackened trunk was hollow. Within the cavity was the rotting corpse of Jack Nolan, still clutching his bag of loot from his employer's house.

Had Jack attempted to hide the loot in the hollow trunk and somehow gotten wedged into the tree, unable to escape? Or had the Devil lured him into a trap? What is certain is that the Devil Tree's sinister reputation kept passersby from investigating the cries that seemed to come out of the cursed tree, so that Jack must have died a slow lingering death of exposure, dehydration, and starvation. Perhaps the Devil's Tree truly was cursed.

The Innkeeper's Frozen Heart

Snow is a funny thing. To some, a heavy snowfall is a very mixed blessing, producing problems to be solved in addition to pleasing the eye by creating a wondrously beautiful landscape. To dairy farmers, it means keeping the cows in the barn and feeding them hay stored from summer. To commuters, it spells extra effort clearing driveways and scraping ice off car windows, while school kids listen expectantly for news of school closings. Generally for Vermonters, snow is good news indeed, for a major winter tourist industry is based on the white stuff. The Green Mountain State boasts nineteen alpine ski resort regions, an amazing number for a relatively small state. The ski season begins at Thanksgiving and can extend well into May with the help of modern snow-making equipment. In Vermont, watching snow fall is like watching dollar bills float gently to earth.

But it was not always thus. A century and a half ago, before ski resorts, snowmobiles or road plows, heavy snows literally were a burden. At least ten feet of snow falls in an average season. A single storm can deposit over thirty inches, and eight-foot drifts are not uncommon. Temperatures can fall to minus 40 degrees Fahrenheit. In the past especially, snowstorms can be killers.

Near Lyndonville, there is an old, half-forgotten story about a winter tragedy that took two lives and, apparently, cursed a country innkeeper as well. It seems that an unexpected blizzard struck the whole state in late March 1873. A mother and her eight-year-old son were forced, by rapidly mounting drifts, to abandon their horse and buggy. They managed to walk three miles, arriving completely exhausted at the door of a small roadside inn.

The innkeeper who answered her knock questioned the woman's judgment in not seeking shelter when the flakes began to fall. "You know how these early spring storms can be," he scolded. "Why did you continue on the road?" "I was hoping to reach our destination," she explained. "My brother's farm lies just south of East Burke, only about four miles further on."

"Besides," she admitted, "I've no money to buy shelter for us, much less the horse." No money was just what the innkeeper didn't want to hear. If he took in mother and child, he might have them as unpaying guests for days until the roads were cleared.

"I've no room," he lied. "You should keep walking—the town center is only half a mile further." It was a heartless refusal. Mother and son staggered off into the blinding blizzard, not to be seen again, at least alive. Two days later, a road crew clearing a huge drift discovered the pair, frozen stiff.

But the tragedy doesn't end there. That August, the selfish innkeeper fell ill. In the midst of a heat wave, he complained of feeling intense cold. His doctor could do nothing, except note his patient's abnormally cold, clammy skin. When death claimed him, his body was extremely cold—almost freezing. The undertaker reported that, in fact, the innkeeper's heart was frozen solid.

The whole community by then knew the story of how the innkeeper had refused shelter to the doomed mother and child that previous winter. The consensus was that the dead man's heart soon would be thawed by the fires of hell.

Dark Denizens of the Deep Woods

Vermont is justly famed for its forests, deep and dark. And these deep woods may hide a dark secret—the Green Mountain State's very own Bigfoot.

Bigfoot, a.k.a. Sasquatch, is alleged to be an apelike creature, usually described as seven or eight feet tall, walking upright, and covered with coarse, dark hair. The creature often is compared with the legendary Abominable Snowman or Yeti, said to roam the slopes of the Himalaya Mountains of Asia.

Bigfoot has been sighted from Oregon to Florida, with most encounters reported in the Pacific Northwest. There is, so far, no indisputable scientific evidence of a large, bipedal ape inhabiting North America. Critics of Bigfoot point out that all known species of great apes—gorillas, orangutans, chimpanzees, and bonobos— are found in tropical forests, not in mid-latitude seasonal environments like the Pacific Northwest or New England. On the other hand, some predominantly tropical species like the Siberian Tiger have successfully spread into much colder environments.

Bigfoot skeptics like to emphasize the improbability of discovery of previously unknown animals on a planet that has been so thoroughly explored. True, early nineteenth-century Europeans at first disbelieved Africans who told about the hairy, upright, man-like "men of the forest"—until, that is, they were convinced of the existence of gorillas. Marine biologist now have proof that gigantic squid, long thought to be the stuff of nightmares, really do exist in the deep. New species of insects, amphibians, and small mammals are being added to the list almost continuously. But could a really large land animal still be unknown? Only a century ago, the okapi, a 500-pound relative of the giraffe, was discovered. The saola, a

primitive hoofed animal, was discovered in Vietnam in 1992. Isn't it arrogant to assume that we've documented scientifically all of earth's creatures?

There is the ecological test—could a mammal as large as Bigfoot find enough food in an environment like Vermont? The answer is, yes of course, if Bigfoot is omnivorous—a plant eater and a meat eater—just like humans. Biologists used to assume that the great apes, humankind's closest relative, genetically, were exclusively plant-eaters. Until, that is, chimps were documented in the wild killing and eating monkeys. Apes also eat termites and other high-protein insects in the wild.

A few Vermonters and visitors have news for the critics: Bigfoot is alive and well in the remote forests of the Northeast Kingdom and, possibly, other rugged parts of the state. Typical of the reported encounters with Bigfoot (how many have gone unreported?) is the experience of a family from New Jersey who were camping near East Haven. It was during "leaf season" and clearly at the end of the outdoor camping calendar. The cold evening suggested a large campfire, which was providing some much-needed warmth in addition to roasting hot dogs and heating a pot of baked beans. The family, who choose to remain anonymous out of fear of ridicule, are convinced that the enticing aroma of cooking food led a Bigfoot toward their campsite.

They first were alerted to the presence of their unwelcome visitor by the stench. Many Bigfoot encounters in the Pacific Northwest have been notable for a strong, unpleasant odor. The East Haven experience was characterized as a "swampy" odor, as of rotting vegetation and marsh gas. Evidently, Bigfoot has not yet advanced to civilized levels of personal hygiene or deodorant use.

Next, bushes and trees began to shake at the edge of the circle of light from the campfire. Then, to their horror, the family members saw two eyes glowing redly in reflected firelight—and those eyes were over six feet above the ground! "Throw more wood on the fire!" shouted the mother, knowing they had not brought weapons. The brighter fire may have discouraged a closer approach by whatever it was. However, in the confusion and near-panic, no one noticed what happened to their food stockpile. They soon discovered that a bag of rolls and a package of marshmallows had gone missing, a small price to pay for a memorable experience.

The Lake Memphremagog Mysteries

There is an old story told up in Newport about a mysterious water monster in Lake Memphremagog. In many ways, Memphremagog is a smaller version of Lake Champlain. Both are long, narrow, and deep. Both cross the international border; while most of Lake Champlain lies within the U.S. with a small portion in Canada, Memphremagog is mostly in Canada with a minor part in Vermont.

Memphremagog is Indian for "beautiful waters," and indeed it is beautiful. But surface beauty often masks danger, and Memphremagog's thirty-two-mile long extent is said to hide a hideous half-man, half-fish creature in its depths. This monster is said to be five to six feet in length covered with slimy dark gray skin and has gills as well as nostrils. It eats fish and is supposed to steal trout and landlocked salmon from fishermen's hooks just as the anglers are reeling in their catch. On at least one occasion, this man-fish (or is it a fish-man?) is said to have come right up on land and helped itself to freshly caught fish stored in a cooler.

Another weird life-form that allegedly makes its home in "Magog," as the locals call the lake, is described as a cross between an alligator and a fish, up to seven feet in length and weighing a hundred pounds. This predator is said to also snatch fish off the hooks of disbelieving anglers, even upsetting small boats in the process.

Is Memphremagog really inhabited by such monsters, or is there some rational explanation for these sightings? Skeptical scientists offer two alternatives to the possibility of unknown, unclassifiable monsters. Their suggestions take away the intriguing mystery of monsters, though, like most such monsters, there is no scientific evidence of their existence in Lake Memphremagog.

The scary man-fish just might be harbor seals. These seals have been known to venture far upstream into freshwater bodies like the St. Lawrence River at Montreal and into Lake Ontario. Some claim to have spotted harbor seals in Lake Champlain. They can be four to six feet long and weigh anywhere from 100 to 300 pounds. They are bold and love fish, lots of fish.

As to the alligatorlike fish, biologists point to lake sturgeon. These definitely live in Lake Champlain, so why not "Magog"? These primitive, and primitive-looking, fish live well over a century. They commonly grow up to six or seven feet in length and weigh over 100 pounds. One was found on a Lake Champlain beach that measured nine feet and 130 pounds! Their rough, bumpy skin gives them the look of an alligator crossed with a barracuda.

So, are the Memphremagog mysteries really some sort of unknown, even prehistoric monsters or merely misdescribed and misunderstood seals or sturgeons? Maybe you should check it out for yourself. At least you might catch some nice fish.

The Candyman

"Sugar season" in Vermont starts with the first milder temperature days in late February or early March. Those are the much-anticipated heralds of spring, when the cycle of freezing and thawing causes the tree saps to rise. As the sap rises in sugar maples, a seasonal industry is resurrected once more. While Quebec is North America's largest producer of maple syrup, Vermont is the top producer in the U.S.

The American Indians taught colonial settlers how to boil down the sap from maple trees, the "sweet water" that flowed in late winter. The Indian technique was to collect the sap oozing from small cuts in the bark, place it in hollowed logs, and drop in hot stones heated in open fires. Gradually, the heat evaporated excess water, concentrating the sweet syrup. The thickening syrup, in turn, can be turned into crystallized sugar. A favorite Indian treat was to pour the syrup onto fresh snow, resulting in a taffylike natural candy.

Watch closely, they say up in the "Northeast Kingdom," and every "sugaring season" you'll see the ghostly figure of an Indian ladle out some warm syrup on packed snow and enjoy the "taffy." You would be seeing the phantom of Great Owl, also known as the Candyman. His is an interesting story from Vermont's Revolutionary War.

Making maple syrup and sugar from the sap of sugar maples is not an easy task, especially using the classic hot stones technique. It takes time. A gallon of maple syrup requires between thirty and fifty gallons of sap. A mature sugar maple will yield about eight gallons of sap, so we're talking about a lot of trees, a lot of sap, and a lot of patience. But the result is worth the effort.

Great Owl became a local legend as a result of his clever deception of British troops trying to locate and confiscate an American weapons cache in the dense woods of northeastern Vermont. Following a moderately successful raid into Canada, American soldiers had retreated into the woods. They decided to hide the cannons and muskets captured in Canada and scatter to their Vermont farms to avoid confronting a larger British force following their trail.

Great Owl was a one man rear guard with a mission to keep the British from finding the hidden weapons. Great Owl decided to allow the British to see him hiding in the woods. On discovery, he pretended to be slow-witted. "Are you looking for the secret?" he asked, all wide-eyed and innocent. "Yes!" was the reply. "Oh, all right, I'll show you the secret—the secret of making candy from trees!" The soldiers, whose diet on the march consisted of salt pork and hard biscuits, were amused but interested. They gathered around as Great Owl demonstrated, ever so slowly, how to tap the trees, boil the syrup down, and make maple taffy by pouring the warm syrup out on fresh snow. The British were so interested in their maple sugar demonstration and in the free samples, that they never did look for the weapons hidden nearby.

Is that the spirit of Great Owl making maple candy in the snow still? Some Vermonters think so.

The Curse on the Healing Waters

Brunswick, Vermont, is a tiny village. Even in a state known for its large number of very small communities, Brunswick appears only on the most detailed maps. It is a mile south of Bloomfield, which likewise doesn't always make the cut when deciding which places to put on the map. Brunswick is located close to the Connecticut River in Essex County, Vermont's northeasternmost county with less than 6,500 inhabitants. Remote and tiny are the key words here.

And yet, Brunswick's mineral spring once was declared the "eighth wonder of the world" by Robert Ripley, whose "Believe It Or Not" accounts of curiosities, natural wonders, mosts, biggests, and firsts, once were syndicated daily in most American newspapers and hundreds of foreign papers as well. Making it into the "Believe It Or Not" column was comparable to repeated exposure on popular TV talkshows—great publicity. Although Ripley gave Brunswick's mineral spring national attention in the 1920s, the springs already had a regional reputation going back several centuries.

The local Indians valued the spring, which actually is six springs all flowing in a tight circle of about fifteen feet in diameter and healing anyone who drank from or bathed in its waters. To the Indians, the waters loaded with iron, sulfur, calcium, and magnesium were a sacred gift from the Great Spirit. Traditionally, the springs were regarded as free and accessible to all tribes and not the exclusive property of any person or group.

European colonists, who came from cultures that also believed in the medicinal properties of mineral springs—a tradition dating back to the Romans—were soon enthusiastic visitors to the spring. As early as the Revolutionary War, entrepreneurs were setting up boarding houses and inns to service travelers searching for cures.

An Indian shaman or medicine man had a warning for these enterprising white men. "You may charge for food and lodging at the spring, but never charge for the waters themselves," he admonished. "This is a wonderful gift from the Great Spirit and must not be the basis for profit. Anyone who charges for these natural medicines will be punished and will not prosper!"

Apparently, early innkeepers honored the principle of unrestricted access and free use. The springs attracted hardy and adventurous travelers to this isolated corner of Vermont and earned a reputation as cures for kidney problems, rheumatism, digestive upset, loss of vitality, and even impotence.

Then the St. Lawrence and Atlantic Railroad came through neighboring Bloomfield. Now the springs were readily accessible to cities from Montreal to Portland, Maine. A local businessman erected a bottling plant to sell the curative water in distant cities. It was struck by lightning, totally destroyed, and never rebuilt. Another ambitious entrepreneur built a hotel at the springs, which he fenced off for the exclusive use of his guests. Lightning struck again, and yet again after that hotel was rebuilt.

In the late 1920s, hoping to capitalize on all the free publicity supplied by "Believe It Or Not," a truly grand hotel was erected, once again restricting the springs to hotel guests only.

Despite a forest of lightning rods on its roof, this one also fell victim to lightning.

Perhaps the warnings about incurring the wrath of the Great Spirit were finally getting through. No one has ever since tried to control access to the healing springs. Should you visit Brunswick Springs, drink up; it's free. Maybe it will even cure what ails you.

The Scalped Ghosts of Memphremagog

Most ghosts are, by definition, scary. But among the most grue-some ghosts anywhere are the scalped ghosts of Lake Memphrema-gog. These fearsome apparitions are said to appear about the time of the first full moon in October every year, commemorating in their fashion a slaughter that occurred in October 1759. This particularly bloody event actually was carried out in revenge for an even more horrific holocaust that same September. And that festival of gore, in turn, was precipitated by the discovery of evidence of wanton bru-tality on the frontier of European settlements in the 1750s in con-nection with the French and Indian Wars.

It used to be assumed that scalping—slicing off the scalp, with attached hair, with a sharp knife and keeping it as a gruesome tro-phy of a slain enemy—was a barbaric custom of Amerindians, who were called savages by the Europeans. Some scholars, however, believe that it was the Europeans who introduced scalping to Native Americans. Whatever the origin, it is a matter of historic record that both the French and the British used to pay bounties to their Amerindian allies for enemy scalps.

The long struggle for control of North America between the mighty empires of France and Britain involved alliances with the Native Americans, hence the term "French and Indian Wars." Before the Europeans appeared, the Iroquois had advanced into Algonquin lands. The French allied themselves with the Algo-nquins, who were happy to help attack the Iroquois. The British, in turn, offered an alliance to the Iroquois.

In 1759, New Englanders under the command of Maj. Robert Rogers, "Rogers Rangers," invaded French Canada to punish Algo-nquins who had raided New England farms and villages. Rogers attacked the Indian village of St. Francis at four in the morning, at first ordering that women and children be spared. But, as dawn broke, light fell on hundreds of white scalps hanging from ceremonial poles. Enraged, the New Englanders slaughtered over 200 men, women, and children, taking their scalps. The Rangers lost only one man.

Algonquin warriors, bent on revenge, pursued the retreating Rangers to the southern end of Lake Memphremagog, where they caught up with one band of Rangers and killed them all, collecting more scalps. Now every October full moon the ghosts of the scalped Rangers stagger on, their white skulls gleaming through the blood that drips down their faces. Still attached to their belts are the bloody scalps of Algonquins that the Rangers earlier had taken as trophies of war. So many scalps. So much blood. So horrific a band of phantoms.

Don't Go in the Attic

The late Victorian house sits on a quiet side street in St. Johnsbury. Although the house looks quite average, it has acquired a dark reputation in the neighborhood. It has had a succession of owners, none of whom have lived there. They rent it, preferably to newcomers who have not heard stories about the resident ghost. Students usually rent rooms in the old house, as Lyndon State College is an easy commute to the north.

The most common experiences with the ghost seem to follow a pattern. At first, nothing unusual happens. Then, after about a week or two, the odd occurrences and weird sounds begin. Lights turn on and off without a human hand in evidence. One student reported that a flashlight equipped with new batteries provided only the dimmest of light within the attic but worked fine elsewhere. Following a quiet grace period of a few weeks, the ghost makes its presence clearer by more activity.

The ghost seems to have the strongest territorial claims to the attic, although conflict with the spirit can occur in other rooms as well. If tenants put their possessions in the attic, they later find them unbroken and carefully placed at the foot of the stairs. Sometimes clothing is even carefully folded—a polite warning that the attic is the ghost's domain. If the students attempt to regain their use of the attic by moving their possessions back up the stairs, then the struggle for occupancy moves on to the next stage—open warfare.

Now things are thrown about violently. Clothes are torn to shreds, toiletries are smashed, papers and books are ripped to pieces. Every material trace of the would-be invader of the attic is destroyed. Once faint and almost imperceptible, the footsteps of the ghost become as noisy as those of a herd of drunken buffalo. Windows and doors open and slam shut. A voice growls, "Stay away! You have no right to be here. No right."

By this time, the most courageous of temporary tenants head for the door. Doubtless, some give serious thought to transferring to the University of California.

The neighborhood gossip speculates that the spirit is a former student at Lyndon State College who may have committed suicide in the attic many decades ago. Supposedly, the young woman was despondent over a broken love affair with her art history teacher and so poisoned herself rather than live on in what had become a cruel world.

Bibliography

Beckley, Timothy. *The UFO Silencers.* New Brunswick, NJ: Inner Light, 1990.

Botkin, B. A., ed. *A Treasury of American Folklore.* New York: Crown Publishers, 1944.

Bryan, Frank, and Bill Mares. *The Vermont Owners Manual.* Shelburne, VT: New England Press, 2000.

Citro, Joseph. *Green Mountain Ghosts, Ghouls and Unsolved Mysteries.* Boston: Houghton Mifflin, 1994.

———. *Green Mountains, Dark Tales.* Lebanon, NH: University Press of New England, 1999.

Clark, Jerome. *Unexplained!* Canton, MI: Visible Ink Press, 1999.

Coleman, Loren. *Mysterious America.* London: Faber and Faber, 1983.

Demos, John. *Entertaining Satan: Witchcraft and the Culture of Early New England.* New York: Oxford University Press, 1982.

Dorson, Richard. *American Folklore.* Chicago: University of Chicago Press, 1959.

Federal Writers' Project. *Vermont: A Guide to the Green Mountain State.* Boston: Houghton Mifflin, 1937.

Guiley, Rosemary. *The Encyclopedia of Ghosts and Spirits.* New York: Facts on File, 1992.

Hauck, Dennis. *Haunted Places: Ghost Abodes, Sacred Sites, UFO Landings, and other Supernatural Locations.* New York: Penguin, 1994.

———. *Haunted Places: The National Directory.* New York: Penguin-Putnam, 2002.

Holzer, Hans. *Yankee Ghosts.* Indianapolis: Bobbs Merrill, 1963.

Jasper, Mark. *Haunted Inns of New England.* Yarmouth Port, MA: On Cape Publications, 2000.

Krantz, Les. *America by Numbers: Facts and Figures from the Weighty to the Way-Out.* Boston: Houghton Mifflin, 1993.

Mack, John. *Abduction: Human Encounters with Aliens.* New York: Scribner, 1994.

Myers, Arthur. *The Ghostly Register.* New York: McGraw-Hill/Contemporary Books, 1986.

Pickering, David. *Casell Dictionary of Superstitions.* London: Casell, 1995.

Pitkin, David. *Ghosts of the Northeast.* New York: Aurora Publications, 2002.

Robinson, Charles. *The New England Ghost Files.* North Attleboro, MA: Covered Bridge Press, 1994.

Skinner, Charles. *American Myths and Legends.* Detroit: Gale Research Company, 1974.

———. *Myths and Legends of Our Own Land: As to Buried Treasure and Storied Waters, Cliffs and Mountains.* Philadelphia: J. B. Lippincott, 1896.

Stein, George, ed. *The Encyclopedia of the Paranormal.* Buffalo, NY: Prometheus, 1996.

Trevor-Roper, H. R. *The European Witch Craze of the Sixteenth and Seventeenth Centuries and Other Essays.* New York: Harper Torchbooks, 1969.

Wead, Doug. *All the Presidents' Children: Triumph and Tragedy in the Lives of America's First Families.* New York: Astria Books, 2003.

Wilson, Harold. *The Hill Country of Northern New England.* New York: Columbia University Press, 1936.

Zarzynski, Joseph. *Champ: Beyond the Legend.* Utica, NY: North Country Books, 1985.

Acknowledgments

THIS IS MY FIFTH BOOK WRITTEN UNDER THE SKILLFUL GUIDANCE AND friendly encouragement of my editor, Kyle Weaver. What always was a good working relationship has developed into a true friendship. As before, Amy Cooper expertly transformed my manuscript into the finished product. Heather Adel Wiggins once again beautifully captured the essence of the stories in her suitably haunting illustrations.

My longtime colleague at Rowan University, Laura Ruthig, expertly word-processed my untidy, handwritten manuscript into usable form; thanks again, Laura.

I wish to thank the many helpful professionals at the Vermont Department of Tourism and Marketing, the Vermont Chamber of Commerce, and the Vermont Attractions Association, all at Montpelier. The knowledgeable staffs at the Vermont Historical Society and Museum in Montpelier, the President Calvin Coolidge State Historic Site, the Bennington Battle Monument, the Ethan Allen Homestead, and Robert Lincoln's Hildene estate all deserve my heartfelt thanks for their expertise and friendly assistance.

My old friend and teaching colleague, Wade Currier, a proud native son of Vermont, introduced me to the beauty and variety of the Green Mountains on a personal field trip many years ago. Wade first acquainted me with the lore and legends of Vermont and introduced me to his cousins who operate local dairy farms and small businesses. It was a memorable introduction to a fascinating state.

My dear wife Diane accompanied me in more extensive fieldwork in Vermont, making a great experience even more enjoyable.

About the Author

CHARLES A. STANSFIELD JR. HAS TAUGHT GEOGRAPHY AT ROWAN University for forty-one years and published fifteen textbooks on cultural and regional geography. In the course of his research, he realized that stories of ghosts and other strange phenomena reflect the history, culture, economy, and even physical geography of a region. He is the author of *Haunted Maine* and *Haunted Jersey Shore* and coauthor with Patricia A. Martinelli of *Haunted New Jersey*. This volume, the second of three focused on the northern New England States, grew out of his long-standing appreciation of the physical and cultural geography of the Green Mountain State.

Other Titles in the
Haunted Series
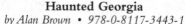

Haunted Georgia
by Alan Brown • *978-0-8117-3443-1*

Haunted Illinois
by Troy Taylor • *978-0-8117-3499-8*

Haunted Kentucky
by Alan Brown • *978-0-8117-3584-1*

Haunted Maryland
by Ed Okonowicz • *978-0-8117-3409-7*

Haunted Massachusetts
by Cheri Revai • *978-0-8117-3221-5*

Haunted New York
by Cheri Revai • *978-0-8117-3249-9*

Haunted New York City
by Cheri Revai • *978-0-8117-3471-4*

Haunted North Carolina
by Patty A. Wilson • *978-0-8117-3585-8*

Haunted Pennsylvania
by Mark Nesbitt and Patty A. Wilson
978-0-8117-3298-7

Haunted Tennessee
by Alan Brown • *978-0-8117-3540-7*

Haunted Texas
by Alan Brown • *978-0-8117-3500-1*

Haunted Virginia
by L. B. Taylor Jr. • *978-0-8117-3541-4*

Haunted West Virginia
by Patty A. Wilson • *978-0-8117-3400-4*

WWW.STACKPOLEBOOKS.COM • **1-800-732-3669**

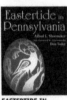